GET BY IN
JAPANESE

**A quick beginners' course for
holidaymakers and business people**

Course writer Chihoko Moran
The Oriental Institute,
University of Oxford
Producer Frank Warwick

BBC Books

Get by in Japanese
A BBC Radio course
First broadcast in Autumn 1987

Published to accompany a series
of programmes prepared in
consultation with the BBC
Educational Broadcasting Council

Acknowledgements

Thanks and appreciation to Kate
Ferguson for her advice and help
in the preparation of this booklet

Illustrations by Julia Rowntree

Published by BBC Books, a division of BBC Enterprises Limited,
Woodlands, 80 Wood Lane, London W12 0TT

ISBN 0 563 21347 7
First published in 1987
Reprinted 1988 (twice)

Printed in England by Belmont Press, Northampton
This book is set in 10 on 11 point Univers Medium

Contents

Introduction

Irasshaimase   That's an expression you will hear frequently in Japan. It means 'welcome – come in', and is used by shopkeepers and others as an invitation as well as a form of greeting.

This book and the accompanying two cassettes, together with the associated radio programmes, extends an invitation to you to learn enough of the Japanese language so that once you've entered you'll be able to 'get by' during a visit or a business trip.

Of course, it's possible to 'survive' in Japan with virtually no knowledge of the language – many restaurants, for example, display remarkably detailed plastic replicas of the dishes in which they specialise, therefore by pointing you can order food and drink. So you won't go hungry. But most of us have other appetites we wish to satisfy; finding your way about the city and countryside, shopping for gifts and souvenirs, changing traveller's cheques, and perhaps above all, engaging in simple everyday conversations that provide insights into the Japanese way of life and enrich your visit.

Get by in Japanese offers a basic 'survival kit' for dealing with these kinds of situations and others that are likely to arise on a visit to Japan and assumes no previous knowledge of the language.

Irasshaimase

Frank Warwick

Frank Warwick, *Producer*

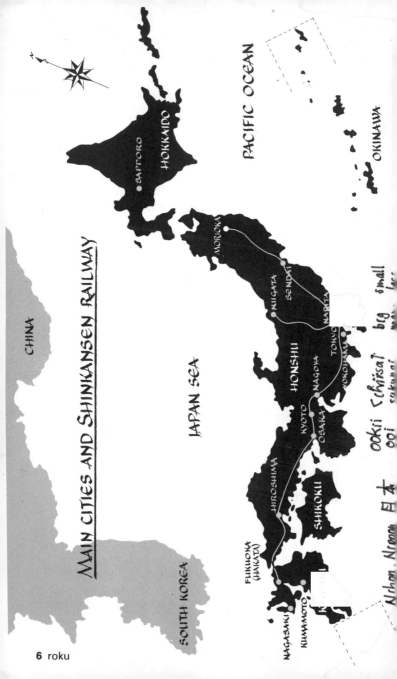

MAIN CITIES AND SHINKANSEN RAILWAY

CHINA

SOUTH KOREA

PACIFIC OCEAN

JAPAN SEA

HOKKAIDO

SAPPORO

HONSHU

MORIOKA

NIIGATA

SENDAI

TOKYO

NARITA

YOKOHAMA

NAGOYA

KYOTO

OSAKA

HIROSHIMA

SHIKOKU

FUKUOKA
(HAKATA)

KUMAMOTO

NAGASAKI

OKINAWA

ōokii [chiisai] big small
ōi chiisai sukunai more less

Nihon, Nippon 日本

Japan

The country and its people

Japan is made up of four principal islands and numerous smaller ones, and lies off the east coast of Asia. Its nearest neighbour, on the Asian mainland, is South Korea, over 100 miles away. It has a slightly larger land area than Britain, but more than three-quarters of it is mountainous and unsuitable for mass habitation and so there is a heavy concentration of population in the coastal areas, mostly to the south and particularly around Tokyo and Osaka. Although most people live away from them the mountains still hold a special place in the heart and spirit of the Japanese, none more so than the truly spectacular Mount Fuji.

Winter in the northern parts of Japan is cold and snowy – skiing is very popular – but where most of the people live the winters are relatively mild. Generally, spring is warm, summer hot and humid, and autumn, the favourite season for many people, beautifully clear and bright. Being further south than Britain, Japan is much hotter in summer and it also has more rain, especially in the 'rainy season' of June and July, and the typhoon season around September.

Japan's history is long, colourful, and well documented, with a literature that goes back more than 1000 years. It was always geographically remote and this isolation from other civilisations was reinforced in the early 17th century when the government decreed that no foreigner could enter Japan and no Japanese could leave it! For over 200 years the country was almost entirely closed to outside influences until the Meiji Reformation in the 1860s when things began to change and

Japan set about the process of 'catching up' with the West — a process that has accelerated since the end of the Second World War to the extent that Japan now has probably the strongest economy in the world.

Buddhism (originally an import from India by way of China) and Shinto (literally 'the Way of the Gods' and native to Japan) figure greatly in the lives of the Japanese and contrary to western ideas of religion, they are not seen to be in competition or contradictory but rather complementary — a kind of balancing of opposing principles. Buddhist temples and Shinto shrines are to be found all over the country, and most Japanese, although they tend to shy away from any open commitment to or discussion of religion, have their wedding ceremony conducted by a Shinto priest and their funeral by a Buddhist.

Whilst Japan with its well-known ability for adaptation has absorbed much from the West, it still remains a more authoritarian society than, say, Britain, with a very strong tradition of respect for seniority, rank and authority, and the language is laced with appropriate expressions of deference. The Japanese usually thinks of himself as a member of a group, which can be the family, the school, the company or organisation for which he works, or even the nation itself. The group provides security and a proper place in the hierarchy. It also demands loyalty and conformity and imposes a sense of duty, and, in contrast to the West, much less is heard in Japan of individuality, independence, privacy and rights.

The course…
and how to use it

About Japanese

Japanese is the native language of about 120 million people in Japan and though it is not an international language like English, the number of people studying it as a foreign language is increasing rapidly, business people being particularly keen.

It is not an especially difficult language to speak and most of the sounds, for English speakers, are relatively easy to reproduce and understand. Japanese should not be confused with Chinese, they are completely different languages, although among the things the Japanese learned from China more than 1000 years ago was the Chinese way of writing. They adapted it to fit their own language, and the resulting writing system is still used today. It is a truly remarkable system and a fascinating study in itself, but much too complex and time-consuming for a short course. In this book we have used a writing system based on the Roman alphabet and although there is more than one way of transcribing or spelling Japanese in 'romanisation', we've chosen the 'Hepburn system' which is by far the most common and also the one most speakers of English find easiest.

Japanese uses many English words and some from other languages and it continues to absorb expressions from abroad. Examples are *passport, hotel, whisky, taxi, limousine, tower, check-out*. (You'll see all of those in lesson 1.) This makes Japanese easier for the English speaker, but remember that these words will be pronounced in a uniquely Japanese way. You may have some difficulty in recognising the word 'limousine', for example, in the Japanese form 'rimujin'; if you say the same word in the ordinary English way the Japanese may have difficulty in understanding you. When speaking Japanese, therefore, be careful to pronounce these 'borrowed' English words in the same way as the Japanese. A guide to pronunciation is given on page 13.

The programmes

- are based largely on specially recorded, real-life conversations, so you get used to hearing everyday Japanese right from the start
- enable you to cope with increasing confidence in day-to-day situations such as meeting people, eating out, shopping, travelling around, booking accommodation and so on
- encourage you to develop a good accent by giving the opportunity to repeat new words and phrases.

The book includes

- an introduction to the sounds of Japanese
- the key words and phrases for each programme
- the texts of the conversations in the order they appear in the programmes
- short explanations of the language
- additional useful vocabulary for each basic situation and background information about Japan and Japanese customs
- a reference section containing extra language notes and vocabulary, numbers, useful addresses and the key to the exercises.

The two cassettes

- contain a condensed form of the programmes and extra conversations and exercises. The key words in the 'Everyday expressions' section are given at the start of cassette 1, so you can hear them and imitate them while getting to know the writing system in the book

- give you the opportunity to go at your own pace, and take your study of the language a stage further if you wish.

To make the most of the course

The way you use the course will depend on you and on whether you're using the cassettes or the programmes or both. Here are some suggestions:

- If you have the cassettes, practise the 'Everyday expressions' given at the start of cassette 1, which are printed on page 15. These provide a useful introduction to the pronunciation as well as being immediately useful

- *Before each programme* look at the key words and phrases at the beginning of each chapter, and practise saying them aloud. Read the conversations aloud several times, with someone else if possible. Check the meaning of any words you don't know with the full word list at the end of the book. Then read the explanations provided

- *During each programme* try to listen to the conversations without looking at the book and concentrate on the sounds of the language. When you're asked to repeat a word or phrase, try saying it aloud and confidently; this will help you to remember the expressions and to pronounce them correctly

- *After each programme* read through the conversations aloud again. If you have the cassettes you may find it useful to imitate the conversations phrase by phrase. On the cassettes the pauses left for you to repeat the words or phrases may seem a little short at first; if so, stop the tape. Check again on the language explanations, then work through the exercises

● Learning a language needs plenty of constant practice – 'little and often' is better than all at once

● When you go to Japan, remember to take this book with you together with a good pocket dictionary.

Guide to pronunciation

Contrary to popular myth, Japanese is easy to pronounce, most of the sounds being very similar to those found in English.

Generally, Japanese is broken up, not so much by vowels and consonants, but rather syllables consisting of a consonant and a vowel.

No syllable is particularly stressed: Japanese give more or less equal weight to all syllables in a word.

The vowels

There are five short vowels and they are pronounced briskly in a rapid staccato way.

a   like the vowel in the English 'bat' but pronounced very flat so that it is also like the *u* sound in 'but'

e   like the vowel in 'bet'

i   like the *ea* in 'beat', but clipped short

o   like the vowel in 'hot', but with lips more rounded

u   like the vowel in 'put', but with lips not rounded.

Long vowels

Vowels with a line above them – e.g. *ā, ō, ū* are pronounced long – double the length you would do normally.

The long vowel *'i'* is usually written *ii* not *ī*. The long vowel *'e'* is usually written *ei* and sometimes *ē*. It is important that the distinction between short and long vowels is made so as to avoid confusion between otherwise identically written words.

When two vowels come together they are pronounced the same way as indicated above so that, for example, the Japanese word *dai* is like the English 'die', though rather clipped and short, and not like the English 'day'.

The consonants

The sounds of consonants are virtually identical to those in English with the following exceptions:

g   is always pronounced hard, as in the English 'giggle', not soft as in 'gentle' or 'gin'

f   is pronounced to sound somewhere between the English *f* and *h*

r   is pronounced almost as if it were *l* (Japanese does not contain a separate *l*) but very quickly and lightly and is never rolled.

Long consonants

Japanese also has long consonants and they are all really pronounced double. For example:

the *kk* in *kekkō* is like the sound in the English 'che**que c**ard' and not like 'check-out'
the *nn* in *'konnichiwa'* is like 'o**ne n**ight' and not as in 'bonny'
the *pp* in *'Nippon'* is like 'ski**p p**ast' and not as in 'skipper'
the *ss* in *'irasshaimase'* is like 'blu**sh sh**yly'.

NB When you listen to the programmes or cassettes you will notice that the sound of *u* seems sometimes to be omitted at the end of words, for example, *desu* (pronounced *dess*). The sound of *i*, too, is frequently omitted, or perhaps whispered. The important thing is to imitate what you hear.

We'll have more to say about pronunciation as we go along.

Everyday expressions

Good morning	*Ohayō* (informal) *Ohayō gozaimasu* (more formal)
Good afternoon/ Good day	*Konnichi wa* (used from late morning onwards)
Good evening	*Konban wa*

NOTE   All the above greetings are used when meeting people, *not* when leaving them.

Good night	*Oyasumi nasai*
Goodbye	*Sayōnara* (used mainly by children) *Jā, mata* (informal) *Shitsurei shimasu* (more formal)
Thank you	*Dōmo* *Arigatō* *Dōmo arigatō* *Dōmo arigatō gozaimasu*

(these all mean the same, but the longer the phrase the more formal it is.)

You're welcome (don't mention it)	*Dō itashimashite*
Please (do, go ahead)	*Dōzo*
Welcome	*Irasshaimase*
Excuse me	*Sumimasen*
Yes	*Hai*
No	*Iie*

1 On arrival

Key expressions

Please (making a polite request)	*Onegaishimasu*
Yes, sir/madam	*Kashikomarimashita*
Yes, it is	*Ē, sō desu*
Is that so?	*Sō desu ka?*
That's fine, it's all right	*Kekkō desu*
What is it?	*Nan desu ka?*
Where is it?	*Doko desu ka?*
How much is it?	*Ikura desu ka?*
Who is it?/ Who are you?	*Donata desu ka?*
	Dare (inf)
What time is it?	*Nan-ji desu ka?*
Here it is	*Kore desu*
It's there	*Soko desu*

(Handwritten annotations: "or 'no thanks' what did you say", "(formal)", "who", "Koro des")

Pronunciation

Long words like *onegaishimasu* and *kashikomarimashita* can be broken up into syllables and then reassembled. Remember to spend an equal amount of time on each syllable, but with no gap between them.

o/ne/ga/i/shi/ma/su

ka/shi/ko/ma/ri/ma/shi/ta

Conversations

At Narita International Airport, Tokyo

CUSTOMS OFFICER Pasupōto wa? *(Passport?)*

MR SMITH Kore desu. *(Here it is)*

CUSTOMS OFFICER	Hai, kekkō desu. *(Yes, that's fine)*
	Onimotsu wa? *(Your luggage?)*
MR SMITH	Kore to sore desu.
	(This one and that one)
CUSTOMS OFFICER	Kore wa nan desu ka?
	(What's this?)
MR SMITH	Uisukii desu. *(It's whisky)*

Outside the arrival lobby

MR SMITH	Rimujin noriba wa doko desu ka?
	(Where is the airport bus stop?)
MAN	Soko desu. *(It's there)*
MR SMITH	Dōmo. *(Thank you)*
MAN	Dō itashimashite. *(You're welcome)*
COACH DRIVER	Kippu wa? *(Ticket?)*
MR SMITH	Kore desu. *(Here it is)*
COACH DRIVER	Hai, dōzo. *(Yes, go ahead)*

Tokyo City Air Terminal

MR SMITH	Takushii noriba wa doko desu ka?
	(Where is the taxi rank?)
RECEPTIONIST	Soko desu. *(It's there)*
MR SMITH	Dai-ichi Hoteru made
	onegaishimasu.
	(To the Dai Ichi Hotel please)
TAXI DRIVER	Dai-ichi Hoteru desu ka?
	(To the Dai Ichi Hotel?)
MR SMITH	Ē, sō desu. *(Yes, that's right)*
TAXI DRIVER	Kashikomarimashita. *(Yes, sir)*
MR SMITH	Are wa nan desu ka? *(What's that?)*
TAXI DRIVER	Tōkyō Tawā desu. *(Tokyo Tower)*
MR SMITH	Ā, sō desu ka? *(Oh, is it?)*

Outside the hotel

MR SMITH	Dōmo arigatō. Ikura desu ka?
	(Thank you. How much is it?)
TAXI DRIVER	San-zen-en desu. *(It's 3000 yen)*
MR SMITH	Hai, san-zen-en. *(Here is 3000 yen)*
TAXI DRIVER	Dōmo arigatō gozaimasu.
	(Thank you very much)

At the hotel reception

RECEPTIONIST Irasshaimase. Donata desu ka?
(Welcome. May I have your name?)

MR SMITH Sumisu desu. *(I am Mr Smith)*

RECEPTIONIST Ā, Sumisu-sama desu ne. Oheya wa san-gai desu. Dōzo. Kochira e.
(Oh yes, Mr Smith. Your room is on the third floor. This way please)

MR SMITH Chōshoku wa nan-ji desu ka?
(What time is breakfast?)

RECEPTIONIST Asa shichi-ji kara ku-ji made desu.
(It's from 7 till 9 in the morning)

MR SMITH Chekkuauto wa nan-ji desu ka?
(What time is check-out?)

RECEPTIONIST Gozen jū-ichi-ji desu. *(It's 11 a.m.)*

Vocabulary

asa *morning*
chekkuauto *check-out*
dai-ichi *number one* (ichi = one; *dai-ichi* = first; *dai-ni* = second, number two)
ē *yes*
en *yen*
-gai *floor*
san-gai *third floor* (Japanese call the ground floor the first floor, so what they call *san-gai*/third floor is two floors up, i.e. the British second floor)
gozen *a.m., morning*
hai *yes*
heya, oheya *room*
hoteru *hotel*
-ji *o'clock, time*
shichi-ji *7 o'clock*
ku-ji *9 o'clock*
jū-ichi-ji *11 o'clock*
nan-ji *what time*
chōshoku *breakfast*
san-zen *3000*
kore *this*

sore *that*
are *that (over there)*
koko *here/this place*
soko *there/that place*
asoko *over there/that place over there*
kochira *this direction/this way*
rimujin *'limousine', private coach, minibus* (e.g. from airport to hotel)
takushii *taxi*
kippu *ticket*
nimotsu, onimotsu *luggage*
noriba *stop* (as in bus stop, taxi *rank*)
pasupōto *passport*
Tōkyō Tawā *Tokyo Tower*
kara *from*
made *till, up to* (can refer to either time or place)
to *and*
Sumisu-san/sama *Mr/Mrs/Miss/Ms Smith*
donata *who*

Explanations

desu is used frequently in Japanese and usually comes at the end of a sentence or clause. It can mean is, am, are, it is, he/she is, we/you/they are, depending on the situation.

Uisukii desu	*It is whisky*
Kore desu	*It is this/this is it*
Kekkō desu	*It is fine/that's okay*
Soko desu	*It is there/there it is*
Tōkyō Tawā desu	*It is Tokyo Tower*
Sumisu desu	*I am Mr Smith*

ka placed at the end of a sentence automatically makes a question. Note that there are no changes in the word order.

Uisukii desu ka?	*Is it whisky?*
Doko desu ka?	*Where is it?*
Nan desu ka?	*What is it?*
Donata desu ka?	*Who is it? Who are you?*
Ikura desu ka?	*How much is it?*

ne, like ka, comes at the end of a sentence and is the equivalent of — isn't it, aren't they, aren't you, etc. It is used when the speaker is confident that the other person will agree with them.

Sumisu-sama desu ne	*You are Mr Smith, aren't you?*
Uisukii desu ne	*It's whisky, isn't it?*

wa is a particle and brings up a topic. The customs officer asks about your passport and luggage, and the coach driver wants to see your ticket.

Pasupōto wa?	*Passport?*
Onimotsu wa?	*Luggage?*
Kippu wa?	*Ticket?*

After you have brought up a topic you can ask or say something about it.

Kore wa *nan desu ka?* starts with *kore* (this).
Kore wa also means 'this', but the *wa* shows that
the customs officer is going to ask or say
something about it. What he wants to know is
Nan desu ka? (What is it?), so he asks What's this?
Kore wa nan desu ka? (This – what is it?)

Mr Smith asks about the coach stop – *rimujin
noriba.* First he brings up the topic, with *rimujin
noriba wa,* then he pops the question, with *doko
desu ka.*

Rimujin noriba wa doko desu ka?
(Where's the coach stop?)

He asks about the taxi rank in the same way.
Takushii noriba wa doko desu ka?
(The taxi rank – where is it?)

From the taxi, the tallest structure in Tokyo
catches his eye, and he asks the driver
Nan desu ka? (What is it?)

Are that (over there). When he raises the topic he
says *Are wa.* He points at it and says
Are wa nan desu ka? (What's that (over there)?/
That over there – what is it?)

Nan-ji desu ka? (What time is it?)
Mr Smith asks about breakfast – *chōshoku.*
Chōshoku wa nan-ji desu ka? (When is breakfast?/
Breakfast – what time is it?)

And he asks about the check-out in the same way.
Chekkuauto wa nan-ji desu ka?

kara, made, e

kara   *from*
made   *(up) to/till*
e   *to (somewhere)*

Like *wa,* all these words come *after* the words they
are connected with, whereas their English
equivalents would come before – *from* Tokyo =
Tōkyō *kara.*

Shichi-ji kara ku-ji made *From 7 o'clock till 9 o'clock*
Hoteru made (or Hoteru e) *To the hotel*
Kochira e *To/in this direction, this way*

-san, -sama

Mr Smith = Sumisu-san, or Sumisu-sama but not when you are talking about yourself.

I am Mr Smith = *Sumisu desu.* This is important so please remember it.

Sumisu-san desu means He is Mr Smith, She is Mrs/Miss/Ms Smith, but it cannot mean I am Mr/Mrs/Miss/Ms Smith (the context will make it clear).

The receptionist calls him *Sumisu-sama.* -sama is the same as -san, but is used mostly in certain kinds of formal relationship, for example to customers in hotels, banks, etc. You will hear -sama used, but you yourself should use -san.

Mr Tanaka *Tanaka-san*
Mr Suzuki *Suzuki-san*

and that is how you should address them.

O-

heya and *oheya* both mean 'room'
nimotsu and *onimotsu* both mean 'luggage'.

O- can be prefixed to many Japanese words, and this is one of the many ways of making speech more polite or formal, less casual or rough. Women are more likely than men to say *onimotsu*, and it is more likely to mean 'your luggage' than 'my luggage' (since you can be more casual about your own things than about other people's).

Japanese often has no exact equivalent of the English 'I', 'you', 'he', 'it', 'they', etc. The same goes for words like 'my', 'mine', 'your', 'yours'. But Japanese has other ways of indicating who it is, or whose luggage etc. it is, that you are talking about.

In the text, *onimotsu* means 'your luggage' and
oheya 'your room'.

Hai

Hai = yes, but it can have other meanings as well.

When the customs officer at the airport looks at
the passport and then says, *Hai, kekkō desu,* the
word *hai* indicates a rather positive, cheerful
attitude. The officer is saying 'Right, that's fine' or
'That's fine, thank you'.

The coach driver has a similar attitude when he
says, *Hai, dōzo.*

Dōzo = please do, go ahead, by all means, on you
go, after you, feel free, help yourself. It is used
when permitting, inviting or encouraging
someone to do something.

Hai, dōzo = yes, on you go, but when the driver
says it he means 'Right you are, on you go', or
'Thank you, go ahead', or 'OK, carry on'.

Additional vocabulary

sochira *that direction, that way*	Narita Kūkō *Narita Airport*
achira *that way, over there*	deguchi *exit*
yūshoku *dinner, evening meal*	kaidan *staircase*
kūkō *airport*	erebētā *lift, elevator*
	tearai, otearai *toilet*
	uketsuke *reception*

Exercises 1

1 Asking what it is

Model

Kore wa nan desu ka?	Uisukii desu
(What's this?)	(It's whisky)

Now you give the answers, using the words in
brackets.

a   Kore wa nan desu ka?   (pasupōto)

b   Kore wa nan desu ka?   (kippu)

Now the answer remains the same, and it's the question that changes.

Model
Sore wa nan desu ka?   Uisukii desu

Now you ask the questions, using the words in brackets.

c   (Kore)   Uisukii desu
d   (Are)   Uisukii desu

2   Asking where it is

Model
Takushii noriba wa   Asoko desu
   doko desu ka?
(Where's the taxi rank?) (It's over there)

Now you give the answers, using the words in brackets.

a   Takushii noriba wa doko desu ka?   (Soko)
b   Takushii noriba wa doko desu ka?   (Koko)

Now the answer remains the same, and it's the question that changes.

Model
Takushii noriba wa   Asoko desu
   doko desu ka?

c   (Rimujin noriba)   Asoko desu
d   (Hoteru)   Asoko desu
e   (Dai-ichi Hoteru)   Asoko desu
f   (Tōkyō Tawā)   Asoko desu

Now you give the answers.

g   Hoteru wa doko desu ka?   (Koko)
h   Hoteru wa doko desu ka?   (Soko)

Using words from the additional vocabulary, you can ask the same kind of questions.

3 Ask the taxi driver to go to ...

Model
Ōkura Hoteru made onegaishimasu
(To the Okura Hotel please)

a (Dai-ichi Hoteru)
b (Tōkyō Tawā)
c (Narita Kūkō)

4 Asking about time

Model
Chōshoku wa nan-ji desu ka?
(What time is breakfast?)

Now ask what time is

a check-out (chekkuauto)?
b dinner (yūshoku)?

Now take the model question, 'Chōshoku wa
nan-ji desu ka?' and make yourself more familiar
with it by filling in the missing word in the
following:

c Chōshoku wa ... desu ka?
d Chōshoku ... nan-ji desu ka?
e Chōshoku wa nan-ji ... ka?
f ... wa nan-ji desu ka?

Worth knowing

If you are arriving in Tokyo on an international
flight you will normally land at Narita International
Airport. Narita is a large modern air terminal and
flight information is given in English as well as
Japanese and many of the airport staff speak
some English so you should have few problems
going through customs and passport control.

The Japan Travel Bureau (Kōtsūkōsha) have an
office, open 24 hours a day, in the main hall at
Narita and it is run by English-speaking staff who
will be only too pleased to help, particularly with

regard to hotel accommodation if you have not made an advance reservation.

To get to Tokyo City itself, by far the best way, other than by taxi which is expensive, is to go by 'Limousine' – a special airport coach service that operates between Narita and Tokyo City Air Terminal and six other destinations within the City.

If your hotel is in one of these six areas of the city, take the 'Limousine' for that destination. If it isn't, or you are unsure, take the 'Limousine' to Tokyo City Air Terminal, TCAT, and then a taxi from there to your hotel. Taxis are the most convenient transportation but they can be expensive. However, no tip is expected and the taxis are comfortable and clean and most have automatic doors and boots which are operated by the driver.

2 Food and drink

Key expressions

What will you have?	*Nan ni nasaimasu ka?* (polite, respectful) *Nan ni shimasu ka?* (commonly used)
I'll have ...	*... ni shimasu*
Please give me ...	*... o kudasai*
Please wait a moment	*Shōshō omachi kudasai*
Excuse me, but ...	*Sumimasen ga ...*
Another cup/glass	*Mō ippai*
It's no good	*Dame desu*
I'd rather have ...	*... ga ii desu*
Do you like ...	*... wa osuki desu ka?*
I like ...	*... ga suki desu*
I like ... very much	*... ga daisuki desu*
What about ... (suggesting something)	*... wa ikaga desu ka?*
It was an excellent meal	*Gochisōsama deshita*

Conversations

In a coffee shop in the morning

WAITRESS   Irasshaimase. Nan ni nasaimasu ka?

CUSTOMER   Tōsuto to jamu o kudasai. Sore kara, kōhii mo onegaishimasu.

WAITRESS   Kōhii o hitotsu to jamu tōsuto o hitotsu desu ne. Kashikomarimashita. Shōshō omachi kudasai.

CUSTOMER	Sumimasen. Kōhii o mō ippai onegaishimasu.
WAITRESS	Hai, tadaima.
CUSTOMER	Sumimasen ga, okanjō onegaishimasu.
WAITRESS	Kashikomarimashita.

What would you like to eat?

MAN	Shokuji o shimashō.
WOMAN TOURIST	Ē, doko e ikimashō ka?
MAN	Nihon ryōri? Chūka ryōri? Soretomo Furansu ryōri?
WOMAN TOURIST	Nihon ryōri ga ii desu.
MAN	Sakana wa osuki desu ka?
WOMAN TOURIST	Ē, niku yori suki desu.
MAN	Osashimi mo tabemasu ka?
WOMAN TOURIST	Mochiron, daisuki desu.
MAN	Jā, sushi-ya e ikimashō.

An afternoon tea party

HOST	Kōcha, kōhii, orenji-jūsu, nani ga ii desu ka?
GUEST	Kōcha o kudasai.
HOST	Kōcha wa, miruku to remon, dochira ni shimasu ka?
GUEST	Remon, onegaishimasu.
HOST	Osatō wa?
GUEST	Futatsu, onegaishimasu.
HOST	Hai, dōzo. Kēki wa ikaga desu ka?
GUEST	Hitotsu itadakimasu. Ā, oishii desu.
HOST	Amai mono ga osuki desu ka?
GUEST	Ē, totemo.
HOST	Kono kēki wa Igirisu no kēki desu.
GUEST	Ā, sō desu ka.

In a restaurant

MAN	Nihon ryōri wa osuki desu ka?
WOMAN	Ē, daisuki desu.
MAN	Koko no tempura wa oishii desu.

WOMAN	Jā, tempura o tabemashō.
MAN	Onomimono wa nan ni shimasu ka? Osake wa ikaga desu ka?
WOMAN	Iya, osake wa dame desu. Biiru ga ii desu.
MAN	Dewa ikimashō ka?
WOMAN	Ē.
MAN	Sumimasen. Okanjō onegaishimasu.
WAITER	Kashikomarimashita. Zenbu de 1340 en desu.
MAN	Kore de onegaishimasu.
WAITER	Dōmo arigatō gozaimashita.
MAN	Gochisōsama deshita.

Vocabulary

biiru *beer*
kōhii *coffee*
orenji-jūsu *orange juice*
sake, osake *rice wine*
ippai *one cup/glass of*
nomimasu *drink, will drink*
nomimono, onomimono
  (a) drink, something to drink
mo *also, too*
mō *another, more*
jamu *jam*
tōsuto *toast*
tempura *deep fried vegetables and fish*
sashimi, osashimi *raw fish*
tabemasu *eat, will eat*
tadaima *straightaway, immediately*
amai *sweet*
dochira *which*
e *to, toward*
itadakimasu *receive, will receive (polite, humble)*
Igirisu *England*
jā *then*
kēki *cake*
mochiron *of course*

mono *thing*
niku *meat*
sakana *fish*
sato, osato *sugar*
shokuji *meal*
soretomo *or*
sushi-ya *sushi shop*
... yori *(more) than ...*
Nihon, Nippon *Japan*
Nihon ryōri *Japanese cooking*
oishii *delicious, tastes good*
gochisōsama *a good meal, an excellent dinner*
kanjō, okanjō *the bill*
zenbu *everything*
... de *at, with, by*
ii *good*
ikimasu *go, will go*
sore kara *and then, after that*
jā *well then*
shimasu *do, will do*
kono *this*
sono *that*
ano *that over there*

Explanations

kudasai please give me

Almost always accompanied with the objects of the request.

Tōsuto o kudasai	*Please give me toast*
Kōhii o kudasai	*Please give me coffee*
Omachi kudasai	*Please wait*
	(Literally, please give me your waiting)

The *o* in the first two examples indicates that the word it follows is the object of the *kudasai* – *o* marks the object.

Kudasai in this context is the same as *onegaishimasu*

Tōsuto o onegaishimasu
Kōhii o onegaishimasu

Note that in conversation *o* is frequently omitted.

Omachi in *omachi kudasai* is not a concrete object, such as *tōsuto* or *kōhii,* and is not followed by *o* nor *onegaishimasu.*

ga comes after the word it is connected with and marks the subject.

Biiru ga ii desu   (Literally, beer is good)

mo also, too

It is placed after the word it is connected with and replaces *wa, ga, o.*

Kore wa kōhii desu (This is coffee)	Kore mo kōhii desu (This is coffee too)
Kore ga kōhii desu (This is coffee)	Kore mo kōhii desu (This also is coffee)
Kōhii o kudasai (Give me coffee please)	Kōhii mo kudasai (Give me coffee too please)

mō another, more

It is placed before the word it is connected with and is often associated with expressions of quantity.

Mō ippai	*Another cup*
Mō ichido	*Once more*
Mō sukoshi	*A little more*

no is a linking word which often corresponds to the English 'in', 'of' and 'from'.

Koko no tempura	*Tempura in this place*
Tōkyō no hoteru	*A hotel in Tokyo*
Igirisu no Sumisu	*Mr Smith from England*

kono, sono, ano

As indicated in chapter 1, there are three words for 'this' and 'that' – *kore, sore* and *are.*

These pronouns can be combined with *no,* to produce the demonstratives, *kono, sono* and *ano.*

Kore (this)	Kono (this, as in 'this coffee')
Sore (that)	Sono (that, as in 'that coffee')
Are (that)	Ano (that, as in 'that coffee over there')

deshita, -mashita

The past tense of *desu* is *deshita* (was/were/has been/have been).

Similarly, verbs ending in *-masu* are placed in the past tense by modifying the ending to *mashita.*

Gochisōsama deshita	*It was an excellent meal*
Arigatō gozaimashita	*Thanks. It was nice of you*
Osake o nomimashita	*I drank/have drunk sake*
Tempura o tabemashita	*I ate/have eaten tempura*

-mashō means 'Let's ...', 'I will do ...' and can be used to modify all verbs ending in -*masu*.

Ikimasu   Ikimashō
            (Let's go/I will go)
Tabemasu   Tabemashō
            (Let's eat/I will eat)

By adding *ka* to *mashō*, you can make a proposal or a suggestion.

Ikimashō ka?   *Shall I/we go?*
Tabemashō ka? *Shall I/we eat?*

de

This particle follows nouns and has a number of different meanings, such as 'at' and 'by'. Here it means 'with'.

Zenbu de   *With everything, in all, altogether*
Kore de   *With this*
Kore de onegaishimasu
             With this (money), please (deal with the bill)

Sumimasen Excuse me/I'm sorry

This can be used to attract the attention of a waiter or shop assistant and is also sometimes used instead of *arigatō gozaimasu*. The ending -*masen* indicates a negative meaning and can be used to modify verbs ending in *masu*.

Tabemasen   *(I) don't eat*
Nomimasen   *(I) don't drink*

Numbers

In Japanese there are two main systems for counting:

The abstract number system – *ichi* (1), *ni* (2), *san* (3) etc. is used for counting in mathematics and for counting scores in games. It is also used for counting things, portions and so on, but in these cases a 'counter' must be added on. For example, if asked how many cups of tea are required you can answer *nihai* (two cups) but you cannot just use the number *ni* (two) by itself. There are many 'counters' in this system and some of those in frequent everyday use are shown separately in the Reference Section on page 83.

A far simpler method of counting things is possible using the *hitotsu, futatsu, mittsu* system which does not require a 'counter' to be added at the end. This system only goes up to ten and is so useful that it merits committing to memory at an early stage. Beyond *tō* (ten), the *ichi, ni, san* system has to be used.

1	*hitotsu*	6	*muttsu*
2	*futatsu*	7	*nanatsu*
3	*mittsu*	8	*yattsu*
4	*yottsu*	9	*kokonotsu*
5	*itsutsu*	10	*tō*

Additional vocabulary

resutoran *restaurant*
kissaten *coffee shop*
mise *shop*
menyū *menu*
sukiyaki *meat and vegetable dish*
yakitori *charcoal grilled chicken*
sarada *salad*
soba, rāmen, udon *kinds of noodles*

hashi, ohashi *chopsticks*
naifu *knife*
fōku *fork*
shio, oshio *salt*
koshō *pepper*
ocha *green tea*
remon tii *lemon tea*
mizu, omizu *water*
kirai *dislikeable*
kanpai! *cheers!, down the hatch!*

Exercises 2

Ordering food

1 The waiter asks what you would like, and you order various things.

Model
Nan ni nasaimasu ka? Kōhii ni shimasu

Nan ni nasaimasu ka?

a   (kōcha) *English tea*   c   (tōsuto) *toast*
b   (orenji-jūsu) *orange juice*   d   (biiru) *beer*

2   This is like exercise 1, but this time your
    answer is a little different.

Model
Nan ni nasaimasu ka?   Kōhii kudasai *or*
                       Kōhii o kudasai

Nan ni nasaimasu ka?

a   (kōcha)   c   (tōsuto)   e   (biiru)
b   (orenji-jūsu) d   (osake)

3   This is like exercises 1 and 2, but again with a
    different answer.

Model
Nan ni nasaimasu ka?   Kōhii o onegaishimasu
                       (the o can be omitted)

Nan ni nasaimasu ka?

a   (kōcha)   c   (tōsuto)   e   (biiru)
b   (orenji-jūsu) d   (osake)

4   **Asking for another cup/glass**

Model
Sumimasen. Kōhii o mō ippai onegaishimasu
(Excuse me. Another cup of coffee please)

Now repeat exactly the same words, changing only
the name of the drink.

a   (kōcha)   b   (orenji-jūsu)   c   (biiru)

5   **Expressing a preference**

Model
Osake wa ikaga desu ka?   Biiru ga ii desu
(What about some sake?) (I'd rather have beer)

a   Biiru wa ikaga desu ka?   (osake)
b   Kōcha wa ikaga desu ka?   (kōhii)

c   Kōhii wa ikaga desu ka?   (kōcha)

d   Takushii wa ikaga desu ka?   (rimujin)

6 Saying whether you like it or not

Model
Nihon ryōri wa osuki desu ka?
(Do you like Japanese cooking?)

Ē, daisuki desu *or* Iie, kirai desu
(Yes, I like it *or* No, I don't like it)

a   Osake wa osuki desu ka?   (daisuki)

b   Kōhii wa osuki desu ka?   (kirai)

c   Kōcha wa osuki desu ka?   (daisuki)

d   Biiru wa osuki desu ka?   (kirai)

7 Declining an invitation or suggestion

Model
Biiru o nomimashō   Sumimasen ga,
                            nomimasen.

Now you decline these suggestions:

a   Kōhii o nomimashō

b   Kōcha o nomimashō

c   Osashimi o tabemashō

d   Nihon ryōri o tabemashō

8 This is the same as exercise 7 but this time you accept the suggestion.

Model
Biiru o nomimashō   Ē, nomimashō.

a   Kōhii o nomimashō

b   Kōcha o nomimashō

c   Osashimi o tabemashō

d   Nihon ryōri o tabemashō

Worth knowing

Eating out is one of the great delights encountered during a visit to Japan and the only real difficulty facing the visitor is one of choice. In every city and town you'll find a huge variety of eating and drinking places – ranging from modest bars serving *sake*, beer and Japanese-style snacks, coffee shops, noisy noodle bars, foreign restaurants, to specialist restaurants that serve just one kind of dish. Many restaurants display in their windows plastic replicas of the dishes they have on offer, together with the price.

Japan has a highly developed fishing industry and seafood, whether eaten raw as in the very popular fish dish *sashimi*, or cooked in a variety of ways, figures prominently in the Japanese cuisine. Meat, particulary beef, is becoming more popular but because of the shortage of home-grown produce, it remains expensive.

The essence of Japanese cuisine is freshness of ingredients combined with great care in the presentation of dishes. Japanese food is prepared so as to appeal as much to the eye as to the palate and many dishes are so delicately decorated that they border on food sculpture.

Whatever the dish, nearly everything is presented in pieces small enough to be eaten in one mouthful. This is, of course, where chopsticks (*hashi*) come into play. Many people argue that to fully appreciate Japanese food it is important to master the technique of handling chopsticks – a skill once learned, never to be forgotten.

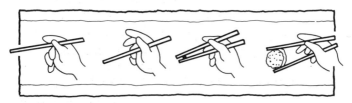

Lager-type beer, whisky and other alcoholic drinks, as well as a range of soft drinks, are widely available in Japan, but the national drink is *sake*. It is a fermented liquor made from rice and is usually served at blood temperature in a small flask and poured into ceramic cups. Its smooth, aromatic taste is quintessentially Japanese and it complements most dishes.

Ocha, green tea, is served generally at the beginning of a meal in a Japanese-style restaurant, and it is also available everywhere at all times. This everyday drinking of *ocha* has little to do with the well-known but little understood tea ceremony which is a rather austere occasion.

The service in most restaurants and bars is quick, efficient and polite and waiters and bar staff do not expect to be tipped although you may find that some restaurants include a service charge.

3 Shopping

Key expressions

How much are you changing?	*Ikura kaemasu ka?*
I'm sorry to have kept you waiting	*Omatase shimashita*
Where do they sell ...?	*... doko de utte imasu ka?*
Show me please	*Misete kudasai*
I/We have it	*Arimasu/Gozaimasu*
I/We haven't got it	*Arimasen/Gozaimasen*
It's just right	*Chōdo ii desu*
I don't want it	*Irimasen*
I'd like (it)/I want (it)	*Hoshii no desu*
It's a little expensive	*Sukoshi takai desu*
Haven't you got a cheaper one?	*Motto yasui no wa arimasen ka?*
I don't understand	*Wakarimasen*
Please write it down	*Kaite kudasai*

Conversations

Before going shopping you need to change some traveller's cheques – *toraberāzu-chekku.*

CUSTOMER	Toraberāzu-chekku o genkin ni kaete kudasai. *(Please cash some traveller's cheques)*
CASHIER	Hai, toraberāzu-chekku wa en desu ka, gaika desu ka?
CUSTOMER	En desu.
CASHIER	Ikura kaemasu ka?
CUSTOMER	Nanaman en onegaishimasu.

CASHIER	Omatase shimashita. Kochira nanaman en desu.
CUSTOMER	Arigatō gozaimashita.

At the store entrance you ask the receptionist where to buy a kimono and a camera.

CUSTOMER	Kimono wa doko de utte imasu ka?
RECEPTIONIST	San-gai desu.
CUSTOMER	Kamera mo utte imasu ka?
RECEPTIONIST	Hai, utte imasu.

When you get to the third floor (*san-gai*) you ask the shop assistant

CUSTOMER	Sumimasen, ano kimono o misete kudasai.
SHOP ASSISTANT	Hai, dōzo.
CUSTOMER	Ikura desu ka?
SHOP ASSISTANT	Ni-man-en de gozaimasu.
CUSTOMER	Sukoshi takai desu. Motto yasui no wa arimasen ka?
SHOP ASSISTANT	Hai, gozaimasu. Kore wa ikaga desu ka?
CUSTOMER	Ikura desu ka?
SHOP ASSISTANT	Ichi-man-go-sen-en de gozaimasu.
CUSTOMER	Wakarimasen. Kaite kudasai.
SHOP ASSISTANT	Hai. *(Writes down 15,000 yen)*
CUSTOMER	Kekkō desu, kaimashō. Obi mo hoshii no desu ga.
SHOP ASSISTANT	Sō desu ne. Kore wa ikaga desu ka?
CUSTOMER	Ii desu ne. Sore o kudasai.
SHOP ASSISTANT	Arigatō gozaimasu. Ryōshūsho ga irimasu ka?
CUSTOMER	Iie, irimasen.

Vocabulary

arimasu *there is/are/exists;* also *I/you/we* etc. *have*
gozaimasu means the same as *arimasu* but is more deferential and more polite
irimasu *(will) need, (will) want* (verb)
misemasu *(will) show* (verb)

kamera	*camera*
fuirumu	*film*
kaemasu	*(will) change,*
	(will) exchange (verb)
urimasu	*(will) sell*
chōdo	*just, exactly*
chiisai	*small*
ōkii	*big*
warui	*bad*
yasui	*cheap*
takai	*high, expensive*
uriba	*selling place or*
	counter in a store or shop
tokei	*clock, watch*
nekkuresu	*necklace*

obi	*a traditional form*
	of sash worn with
	a kimono
yubiwa	*ring for the finger*
pondo	*pound sterling*
hyaku pondo	*£100 sterling*
doru	*dollar*
satsu	*note in currency*
ichi-man-en-satsu	
	a ¥10,000 note
-mai attached to numbers
(*ichi-mai, ni-mai,*
san-mai etc.) when
counting flat things,
e.g. sheets of paper

Explanations

The polite request – the **-*te*** form of verbs followed by *kudasai*.

Most of the verbs we have used up to now have been based on the -*masu* form, e.g. *ikimasu, tabemasu, nomimasu* and so on. When you wish to politely ask someone to do something for you, it is important that you use the -*te* form followed by *kudasai*. Sometimes the -*te* form is simply the verb with the ending -*te* in place of -*masu*, but this is not always the case and occasionally -*de* is used. At this stage it will be easier to memorise the following frequently used verbs with their -*te* form.

VERB		-TE FORM	PLEASE ...
misemasu	*show*	misete	misete kudasai
kaemasu	*change*	kaete	kaete kudasai
urimasu	*sell*	utte	utte kudasai
ikimasu	*go*	itte	itte kudasai
tabemasu	*eat*	tabete	tabete kudasai
nomimasu	*drink*	nonde	nonde kudasai
kakimasu	*write*	kaite	kaite kudasai
kaimasu	*buy*	katte	katte kudasai

At what place do they sell ...?

The -te form of verbs followed by *imasu ka?* is also used when you ask this kind of question. Conversation 2 starts with:

Kimono wa doko de utte imasu ka?
(Kimonos – where do they sell them?)

and you will note that the topic, *kimono*, is raised first and is followed by the question.

If the answer to this question is negative the response would be:

Kimono wa koko de utte imasen
(Kimonos – they don't sell here)

Note that the negative form of *imasu, imasen* is used and *ka* is omitted. *Koko* (here) replaces *doko* (where).

Singular and plural

Most nouns in Japanese appear in one single form although the context will usually indicate where the noun is singular or plural.

Kamera wa doko de utte imasu ka?
(Where do they sell cameras?)

Sono kamera o misete kudasai
(Please show me that camera)

Asking for something different

Sukoshi *takai* desu
(It's a little *expensive*)

Motto *yasui* no wa arimasen ka?
(Haven't you got anything cheaper?)

Can be used with various combinations of opposite adjectives by simply substituting them for *takai* and *yasui.*

> Sukoshi takai desu.
> Motto yasui no wa arimasen ka?

chiisai	*small*	ōkii	*big*
warui	*bad*	ii	*good*
mijikai	*short*	nagai	*long*
omoi	*heavy*	karui	*light*
furui	*old*	atarashii	*new*
kitanai	*dirty*	kirei na	*clean*
hade	*loud*	jimi na	*subdued*

no as a pronoun

Yasui no   *A cheap one*
Takai no   *An expensive one*

but this *no* should not be confused with the linking *no* which means 'of'.

de gozaimasu is the same as *desu,* but it shows the speaker is being particularly polite.

Additional vocabulary

genkin *cash*
gaika *foreign currency*
miyage, omiyage *souvenir, gift*
hagaki *postcard*
kitte *postage stamps*
yūbinkyoku *post office*
mijikai *short*
nagai *long*
karui *light*
omoi *heavy*
furui *old*
atarashii *new*

kitanai *dirty, soiled*
kirei (na) *clean, beautiful*
hade (na) *loud*
  (colour or style)
jimi (na) *subdued*
  (colour or style)
yukata *informal cotton robe, 'kimono' (see note on page 44)*

Exercises 3

1   Please change ... into yen

Model
Toraberāzu-chekku o en ni kaete kudasai
(*clue* toraberāzu-chekku)

a   (pondo)

b   (doru)

c   (hyaku-pondo)

d   (go-hyaku-doru)

e   (toraberāzu-chekku)

2 Where do they sell ...?

Model
Tokei wa doko de utte imasu ka?
(*clue* tokei)

a (kimono)   d (fuirumu)
b (kamera)   e (nekkuresu)
c (kippu)

3 Show me that ...

Model
Kimono o misete kudasai
(*clue* kimono)

a (tokei)   d (sono nekkuresu)
b (kore)   e (ano kimono)
c (ano kamera)   f (kono yubiwa)

4 Have you got a better/bigger/cheaper/dearer one?

Model
Motto ii no wa arimasen ka?
(*clue* ii)

a (chiisai)   c (yasui)
b (ōkii)   d (takai)

5 Say it in Japanese

a Where do they sell kimonos?
b Show me that kimono
c Isn't there a cheaper one?

The casual cotton robe which has become known in English as kimono is actually called *yukata* in Japanese. The word *kimono* in Japanese is reserved for more formal and much more expensive garments worn by both men and women.

Worth knowing

Banks are perhaps the best and quickest way to exchange money and traveller's cheques although some leading hotels and stores are also authorised currency exchanges and can be useful outside banking hours. Remember to take your passport *(pasupōto)* with you. Banks are open

> Weekdays 9.00 a.m. – 3.00 p.m.
> Saturdays 9.00 a.m. – 12.00 p.m. *(except for the second Saturday in every month)*

Japan's currency unit is the Yen (¥). The bank notes in common use are 500, 1000, 5000 and 10,000 and there are also coins in units of 1, 5, 10, 50, 100 and 500.

Most shopping in Japan is done in the many large department stores *(depāto)* and they offer a vast range of goods and services including good inexpensive restaurants. Although such stores are frequently crowded the service is prompt and polite and purchases are usually beautifully wrapped by the sales assistant. Department stores are also the easiest places to find a public toilet *(otearai)*.

Much smaller shops, selling traditional craft items, souvenirs and attractive gifts, are to be found in the small narrow streets of the downtown areas of most cities.

In Tokyo, away from the big department stores, there are particular areas where specialised goods are sold, often at bargain prices. The most notable, perhaps, is Akihabara, where you will find a bewildering array of the latest electronic equipment.

4 A trip to Kyoto

Key expressions

Please give me/I'll receive
Please let me (have, do etc.)
With your permission,
I'll have, do etc.   *itadakimasu*

I want to go to (Kyoto)   *(Kyōto) e ikitai no desu*

One ticket to (Kyoto)   *(Kyōto-yuki) no kippu o*
please   *ichi-mai onegaishimasu*

Where does the Bullet   *Shinkansen wa doko*
Train leave from?   *desu ka?*

What time does it arrive   *(Kyōto) ni nan-ji ni*
(at Kyoto)?   *tsukimasu ka?*

Please turn to the left   *Hidari ni magatte*
                                   kudasai

Please turn to the right   *Migi ni magatte kudasai*

Please repeat it/   *Mō ichido itte kudasai*
Say it again

I understand/I see/Right   *Wakarimashita*

How much is it for one   *Hitoban ikura desu ka?*
night?

After you/Excuse me for   *Osaki ni*
going before you

What will you do?   *Dō shimasu ka?*
                                   Dō nasaimasu ka?
                                   (more polite)

Conversations

Buying a ticket at the railway station

TRAVELLER   Kyōto-yuki no kippu o ichi-mai
                 onegaishimasu.

CLERK	Ittō desu ka?
TRAVELLER	Iie, nitō desu.
CLERK	Katamichi desu ka?
TRAVELLER	Iie, ōfuku o onegaishimasu.
CLERK	Shitei-seki ga irimasu ka?
TRAVELLER	Irimasen. Jiyū-seki de ikimasu.
CLERK	Jā, jōsha-ken to tokkyū-ken. Ichi-man-go-sen-en itadakimasu.
TRAVELLER	Hai, ni-man-en.
CLERK	Go-sen-en no otsuri desu.
TRAVELLER	Arigatō.

From which platform does the train leave?

TRAVELLER	Shinkansen wa doko desu ka?
CLERK	Shinkansen no hōmu wa jū-yon-ban-sen kara jū-kyū-ban-sen desu. Kono tsūro o massugu itte, Yaesu-guchi o hidari ni magatte kudasai.
TRAVELLER	Sumimasen ga, mō ichido itte kudasai.
CLERK	Shinkansen no hōmu wa jū-yon-ban-sen kara jū-kyū-ban-sen desu. Kono tsūro o massugu itte, Yaesu-guchi o hidari ni magatte kudasai.
TRAVELLER	Wakarimashita. Arigatō.

What time does the train leave?

TRAVELLER	Kyōto e ikitai no desu ga, tsugi no densha wa nan-ji desu ka?
CLERK	Tsugi wa jū-san-ji hatsu ga gozaimasu.
TRAVELLER	Jū-san-ji desu ne.
CLERK	Hai, sō desu.
TRAVELLER	Kyōto ni nan-ji ni tsukimasu ka?
CLERK	Jū-go-ji-go-juppun desu.
TRAVELLER	Wakarimashita. Dōmo arigatō.
CLERK	Iie, dō itashimashite.

Finding a room at the inn (ryokan)

TRAVELLER	Konban heya ga arimasu ka?
INNKEEPER	Ohitori desu ka?
TRAVELLER	Ē.
INNKEEPER	Hai, gozaimasu.
TRAVELLER	Hito-ban ikura desu ka?
INNKEEPER	Chōshoku-tsuki de hassen-en desu.

The innkeeper shows you to your room

INNKEEPER	Dōzo. Kochira e. Oheya wa ni-kai desu.
TRAVELLER	Hiroi desu ne. Ofuro wa doko desu ka?
INNKEEPER	Ikkai desu.
TRAVELLER	Otearai wa?
INNKEEPER	Rōka no tsukiatari desu. Konban, yūshoku wa dō nasaimasu ka?
TRAVELLER	Soto de tabemasu.

Leaving the ryokan to have a look round the town

TRAVELLER	Chotto itte kimasu.
INNKEEPER	Sō desu ka. Dochira e?
TRAVELLER	Machi ga mitai no desu.
INNKEEPER	Okyaku-san, Kyōto wa hajimete desu ka?
TRAVELLER	Sō desu.
INNKEEPER	Itte irasshaimase.

On your return ...

TRAVELLER	Tadaima.
INNKEEPER	Okaerinasaimase.

Vocabulary

Kyōto-yuki *Kyoto-bound* (train etc., for Kyoto)	hiroi *wide, large*
hidari *left*	semai *narrow, small*
migi *right*	hitori, ohitori *one person*
massugu *straight*	rōka *corridor*
tsugi *next*	machi *town*
	okyaku-san *client, customer*

Words connected with transport

basu	*bus*	ittō	*first class*
kuruma, jidōsha	*car*	nitō	*second class*
fune	*ship*	katamichi	*single ticket*
ferii	*ferry boat*	ōfuku	*return*
jitensha	*bicycle*	jōsha-ken	*ordinary ticket*
hikōki	*aeroplane*	tokkyū-ken	*super express*
takushii	*taxi*		*ticket*
chikatetsu	*underground*	shindai-sha	*sleeping berth*
esukarētā	*escalator*	shokudō-sha	*dining car*
eki	*station*	kin-en-sha	*non-smoking*
densha	*train*		*car*
Shinkansen	*Bullet Train*	shitei-seki	*reserved seat*
tokkyū	*super express*	jiyū-seki	*unreserved seat*

Explanations

Position of ichi-mai etc. with onegaishimasu

Note that words indicating quantity – *ichi-mai, ippai, ichi-en* etc., in a request, come before *onegaishimasu*. Hence:

Kyōto-yuki no kippu o *ichi-mai* onegaishimasu.

Shiteiseki ga irimasu ka?

Literally this means 'Is a reserved seat necessary?' with *ga* indicating the subject. But in this context it means 'Do you want a reserved seat?'

Ichi-man-go-sen-en itadakimasu

Although *itadakimasu* means 'I receive', it is also a polite way of implying both acceptance and gratitude. Therefore in this context it means 'May I respectfully ask you for 15,000 yen' or '15,000 yen, if you don't mind, sir.'

The -*te* form of ikimasu (go) and that of *iimasu* (say) are the same – *itte*. The context will make clear the intention; e.g. massugu itte (go straight), mō ichido itte kudasai (please say it again).

...*e* means 'to....'

Kyōto e	*to Kyoto*
Tōkyō eki e	*to Tokyo station*
Doko e?	*to where/where to?*

The -*te* form of a verb can connect two sentences in much the same way as 'and' in English. It can also link several sentences together, like 'and then'; as in:

Hoteru o *dete*, migi ni *magatte*, tsugi no kado o hidari ni *magatte*, massugu ikimasu
(Go out of the hotel and turn right, and then at the next corner you turn left then go straight ahead)

The idea of desiring or wanting a course of action is expressed by replacing the -*masu* verb ending with -*tai*.

Kaimasu (buy)	Kaitai no desu (I want to buy)
Ikimasu (go)	Ikitai no desu (I want to go)

Hiroi means 'wide', but is also used to mean 'large' when talking about areas. Narrow – small in area – is ***semai***.

Dō nasaimasu ka? is a respectful way of asking what someone is going to do or how they are going to do it. It is more polite than *dō shimasu ka?*

Itte kimasu; itte irasshaimase

When you leave the house or leave the office, a fixed phrase is used – *Itte kimasu*, which literally means 'going, I'll come back'. The standard response by those left at home or in the office is *Itte irasshai* or more deferentially, *itte irasshaimase*.

Tadaima; okaerinasai (mase)

When you return to home or office there is again a fixed phrase. You call out *tadaima*, to which the normal response is *okaerinasai* or more politely, *okaerinasaimase*.

Okyaku-san means 'customer'

In place of the English 'you', Japanese often uses a title such as *sensei* for teacher or doctor, or the person's name, e.g. *Suzuki-san*. So that when the innkeeper is speaking to his customer he says,

Okyaku-san, Kyōto wa hajimete desu ka?
(Is this the *customer's* first time in Kyoto?)

Exercises 4

1 Where do you want to go?

Model
Tōkyō eki e ikitai no desu
(I want to go to Tokyo station)

What would you say if you wanted to go to

a Kyōto?　　b Ginza?　c Hiroshima?

2 Being given directions

Model
Yaesu-guchi o *hidari* ni magatte kudasai
(Turn *left* at the *Yaesu exit*)

Yaesu-guchi o *migi* ni magatte kudasai
(Turn *right* at the *Yaesu exit*)

Now say turn

a left at the next corner *(tsugi no kado)*

b right at the next corner

c left there *(soko)*

d right there

e left at that corner over there

f right at that corner over there

3 Buying a ticket

Model
Kyōto-yuki no kippu o ichi-mai onegaishimasu
(One ticket to Kyoto please)

Now ask for a ticket to

a   Ōsaka   c   Hiroshima
b   Kōbe   d   Fukuoka

4   Is there...?

Model
Heya ga arimasu ka?   (Is there a room?)

Now ask if there is

a   a telephone?   (*denwa*)
b   a television?   (*terebi*)
c   a newspaper?   (*shinbun*)
d   a radio?   (*rajio*)
e   a shower?   (*shawā*)

5   How much is...?

Model
Heya wa *hitoban* ikura desu ka?
(How much is a room for one night?)

Now ask how much is

a   one cup of coffee?
b   one ticket?
c   one kimono?
d   a ticket for one on the limousine?

6   The maid at the *ryokan* says the following in response to what you said. What did you say?

a   'Itte irasshaimase'   b   'Okaerinasai'

Worth knowing

For many visitors to Japan, Kyoto comes very high on their list of places to see and explore. It was the capital of the country for more than 1000 years until 1868 when the Edo period came to an end and the Emperor Meiji established his new capital at Tokyo.

Kyoto symbolises the tradition and splendour of Japan's ancient culture and its hundreds of Shinto shrines and Buddhist temples, immaculate landscaped gardens, art treasures, and folk crafts are a continuing attraction.

The most convenient way to get from Tokyo to Kyoto, and indeed to all other major cities, is by train. Japan has one of the most efficient railway systems in the world and if you are planning to make several journeys throughout the country it is advisable to purchase a Japan Rail Pass *before* you arrive in Japan as this can produce considerable savings in rail fares.

The most famous rail service is the *Shinkansen*, the 'Bullet Train', which has been running between Tokyo and Osaka since 1964, and now goes as far as Hakata to the west and Morioka in the northeast. The faster *Shinkansen* trains are called *Hikari* (lightning) and the others which stop at more stations but still travel extremely fast are *Kodama* (echo).

There are also some private railway lines and other local lines serving urban areas and whilst they are equally efficient they are perhaps best avoided during the busy rush hours.

Long distance trains usually have restaurant or buffet cars and the standard of food is high, as is the service. Also available on trains and at most mainline stations are lunch boxes – *Bentō* – that contan rice, pickles, an assortment of vegetables, fish, meat and eggs, all packed in attractive wooden boxes.

Luggage space is limited on trains and coin-operated luggage lockers on station platforms only accept small suit-cases. So the key to enjoyable rail travel is to travel light.

Ryokan – Japanese-style Inn

A trip to Kyoto provides a good opportunity to stay in a *ryokan*, a Japanese-style inn. A *ryokan* gives the chance to experience the customs and manners of the traditional Japanese lifestyle, starting from the moment you arrive when you must take off your shoes. You'll sleep on a comfortable mattress, *futon*, laid out on the floor of a *tatami* straw matted room which serves as a living room during the day. Dinner and breakfast, usually served in the room, are authentic Japanese-style dishes and the service is delicate and refined. Bathrooms are Japanese-style and often communal although there are separate baths for men and women. The bath (*furo, ofuro*) is deep and the water very hot and *not* for washing in – you wash and rinse thoroughly *before* entering the bath, using the basins and taps.

A feature of many *ryokan* is the very fine gardens, traditionally laid out with imaginative use of water to create a relaxed atmosphere. *Ryokan* are not for the man in a hurry, and privacy is not their strong point, but their unique charm is such that it is not hard to see why many visitors prefer them.

Dining out

Kyoto has a distinctive cuisine, noted especially for the light use of seasonings combined with a wide variety of vegetables. Originally *Kyō ryōri* – Kyoto-style cuisine – had three styles – *Yosuku ryōri* – dishes for court people: *Kaiseki ryōri* – a meal served before the tea ceremony: and *Shōjin ryōri* – vegetarian dishes for Buddhist priests. Today Kyoto-style cuisine also features fish, soups, rice and a variety of main dishes, chosen according to season. *Kyō ryōri* dishes in top-class restaurants can be expensive. However, the essence of Kyoto cuisine can be enjoyed by sampling a *Kyō bentō* – a Kyoto-style lunch box.

Kyoto is also famous for *Tōfu* – soya bean curd, a particularly nutritious food, that is prepared in a wide variety of ways.

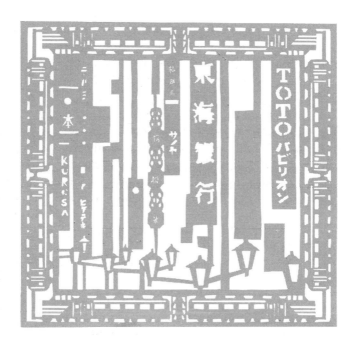

5 Out and about

Key expressions

What are you going by?	*Nan de ikimasu ka?*
That would be a good idea	*Sore wa ii kangae desu.*
The (subway) is the most convenient	*(Chikatetsu) ga ichiban benri desu*
Why (is it so)?	*Dōshite (desu ka)?*
Is it near/far?	*Chikai/tōi desu ka?*
It's (5 minutes') walk	*Aruite (go-fun) desu*
How long does it take?	*Dono gurai kakarimasu ka?*
Don't smoke please	*Tabako o suwanai de kudasai*
What time is it open from?	*Nan-ji kara aite imasu ka?*
It closes at (5.00 p.m.)	*(Go-ji) ni shimarimasu*
I've lost my way	*Michi ni mayoimashita*
I'm in trouble	*Komarimashita*
Has it already left?	*Mō demashita ka?*
It can't be helped	*Shikata ga arimasen*

Conversations

A visit to the temple, Asakusa Kannon, in Asakusa

MAN	Asakusa Kannon e ikimasen ka?
WOMAN	Sore wa ii kangae desu ne. Koko kara nan de ikimasu ka?
MAN	Chikatetsu ga ichiban benri desu.
WOMAN	Dōshite desu ka?
MAN	Norikae ga arimasen. Shibuya-eki kara Ginza-sen ni notte Asakusa de orimasu.

WOMAN	Sore wa kantan desu ne. Otera wa Asakusa kara chikai desu ka?
MAN	Aruite go-fun desu.
WOMAN	Shibuya-eki kara Asakusa made chikatetsu de dono gurai kakarimasu ka?
MAN	Yon-juppun kakarimasu.
WOMAN	Tōi desu ne.

How much does it cost to enter?

MAN	Haikanryō wa ikura desu ka?
RECEPTIONIST	Otona hyaku-en, kodomo go-jū-en desu.
MAN	Otona ni-mai kudasai.
RECEPTIONIST	Hai, dōzo. Naka de tabako o suwanai de kudasai.

Opening hours

MAN	Otera wa nan-ji kara aite imasu ka?
RECEPTIONIST	Jū-ji kara aite imasu.
MAN	Nan-ji ni shimarimasu ka?
RECEPTIONIST	Go-ji ni shimarimasu. Nichi-yōbi wa roku-ji made desu.

Going home

MAN	Komarimashita. Michi ni mayoimashita.
WOMAN	Asoko no omawari-san ni tazunemashō.
MAN	*(to policeman)* Sumimasen ga, eki wa dō ikimasu ka?
POLICEMAN	Asoko ni kōsaten ga arimasu. Soko o migi ni magarimasu. Sukoshi ikimasu to tabako-ya ga arimasu. Soko o migi ni magatte sugu hidari ni hairimasu. Sono tsukiatari ga eki desu.

At the station

MAN	Shūden wa mō demashita ka?
STATION MASTER	Ē, ima demashita.
WOMAN	Shikata ga arimasen. Takushii de kaerimashō.

Vocabulary

kangae *idea*
ichiban *the most, first*
benri *convenient*
norimasu, notte, noranai *get on*
orimasu, orite, orinai *get off*
norikae *change*
tera, otera *temple*
chikai *near*
tōi *far*
arukimasu, aruite, arukanai *walk, by foot*
kakarimasu, kakatte, kakaranai *take, cost*
de *by (means of)*
fun, pun *minute(s)*
shikata *way, method*
nyūjōryō, haikanryō *entrance fee*
otona *adult*
kodomo *child*
suimasu, sutte, suwanai *smoke*
akimasu, aite, akanai *open*
shimarimasu, shimatte, shimaranai *shut, close*

nichi-yōbi *Sunday*
komarimasu, komatte, komaranai *be in trouble*
michi *path, road*
mayoimasu, mayotte, mayowanai *lose one's way*
omawari-san *policeman*
tazunemasu, tazunete, tazunanai *ask*
kōsaten *junction*
tabako-ya *tobacconist*
hairimasu, haitte, hairanai *enter*
tsukiatari *end (of a passage, road)*
shūden *last train*
demasu, dete, denai *leave*
kantan *simple*
eiga *film, movie*
dōbutsu-en *zoo*
hayai *fast*
mimasu, mite, minai *see*
fuyu *winter*
samui *cold*

Explanations

Ikimasen ka? Wouldn't you like to go?

This type of negative question is often used in conversation as a polite invitation. It can also mean 'Don't you go?' depending on the content.

Nan de ikimasu ka? What are you going by?

This asks what kind of transportation will be used. See explanation below for *Aruite go-fun desu.*

Chikatetsu ga ichiban benri desu

When comparing three or more things and regarding one of them (A) as superior, inferior etc. to the others, the pattern of the sentence is:

(A) ga ichiban (B) desu.

Tōkyō ga ichiban ii desu
Tokyo is the best

Shinkansen ga ichiban hayai desu
The Bullet Train is the fastest

Fuyu ga ichiban samui desu
Winter is the coldest.

Aruite go-fun desu

Aruite is the *-te* form of *arukimasu* and means 'by walking'. Please note, however, that when describing the form of transport, i.e. 'by car', 'by train', 'by bus', you use the name of the transport followed by *de*.

Kuruma de go-fun desu
(It takes 5 minutes by *car)*

Densha de go-fun desu
(It takes 5 minutes by *train)*

Basu de go-fun desu
(It takes 5 minutes by *bus)*.

Dono gurai kakarimasu ka? in the first
conversation means 'How long does it take?'

However it can also mean 'How much does it cost?' and although the context will usually make it clear what is intended there are occasions when confusion is unavoidable, even among Japanese.

Haikanryō is the entrance fee for temples, shrines
and the like.

Admission fees for other places such as theatres, exhibitions, fairgrounds etc. is *nyūjōryō*.

Aite imasu   **'It's open'**
Aite imasu ka   'is it open?', 'Is it vacant?',
                          'Is it free?'

Aite is the *-te* form of *akimasu*.

The *-te imasu* form has various meanings. The most common and easiest to understand, is the 'is doing' meaning, e.g:

Nani o shi*te imasu* ka?   (What are you doing?')/
                                    ('What is he doing?')

Gohan o tabe*te imasu*   ('He (she) is eating rice/
                                    dinner')

Note *gohan* means cooked rice but it also means food/dinner/a meal.

But the *-te imasu* form also has other meanings, as in:

aite imasu, which means 'It's open' (not 'it is opening') or *utte imasu*, which means 'they sell' more often than 'they are selling' (see Chapter 3) or *kaette imasu,* which means 'he (she) has come back' not 'is coming back'

Mō demashita ka?   **'Has it already left?'**

mō followed by the past tense of a verb means 'it has already been done.', e.g:

mō tabemashita ka?   Have you already eaten
                                  (it)?
Hai, *mō* tabemashita   'Yes, I have (eaten it)'
Mō mimashita ka?   'Have you seen (it)?'
Hai, *mō* mimashita   'Yes, I have (seen it)'

Note This *mō* is different from *mō ippai*, *mō ichido, mō sukoshi* (see Chapter 2).

Tabako o suwanai de kudasai

The core of a verb combined with *nai de kudasai* expresses a polite negative request. The verb 'to smoke' is *suimasu* whilst 'do not smoke' is *suwanai*. There are four variations on the manner of combination of the core of a verb with *nai*:

Ikimasu (go)	Ikanai de kudasai (Please don't go)
Tabemasu (eat)	tabenai de kudasai (Please don't eat)
Mimasu (see)	minai de kudasai (Please don't look)
kimasu (come)	konai de kudasai (Please don't come).

Sukoshi ikimasu to tabako-ya ga arimasu

... *to* ... connects two sentences and implies that the second sentence is a necessary or unavoidable or immediate consequence of the first sentence.

Hidari ni magarimasu to Tōkyō Tawā ga arimasu
(You turn to the left and there's Tokyo Tower)

Massugu ikimasu to eki desu
(You go straight and there's the station)

Fuyu ga kimasu to samui desu
(When the winter comes it's cold).

Additional vocabulary

haru	*spring*	jinja	*shrine*
natsu	*summer*	yūbinkyoku	*post office*
aki	*autumn*	ginkō	*bank*
garō	*art gallery*	annaisho	*guide book*
shiro	*castle*	katarogu	*catalogue*
shinai	*downtown area*	gekijō	*theatre*
ichiba	*market*	eigakan	*cinema*
hakubutsukan	*museum*	konsāto-hōru	*concert hall*
kōen	*park*	naito kurabu	*night club*
Kōkyo	*Imperial Palace*		

Exercises 5

1 Asking someone if they would like to go somewhere.

Model
Asakusa Kannon e ikimasen ka?
(Wouldn't you like to go to *Asakusa Kannon*?)

a Kamakura?
b Eiga? (film)
c Sukii? (skiing)

2 Asking someone if they would like to do something.

Model
Ikimasen ka?
(Wouldn't you like to go?)

a to eat?
b to drink?
c to see?

3 The best way

Model
Chikatetsu ga ichiban benri desu
(The subway is the most convenient)

a the fastest
b the nearest
c the cheapest

4 How far is it?

Model
Aruite go-fun desu
(It's 5 minutes' walk)

a 10 minutes
b 4 minutes
c 2 minutes

5 How long does it take?

Model
Tōkyō kara Kyōto made dono gurai
    kakarimasu ka?
(How long does it take from Tokyo to Kyoto?)

a   from the station to the hotel
b   from here to there
c   from the temple to the station

6 Please don't ...

Model
Tabako o suwanai de kudasai
(Please don't smoke)

a   drink sake
b   see a film
c   eat sashimi

7 Is it open ...?

Model
Otera wa aite imasu ka?
(Is the temple open?)

Ask if the following are open

a   department store
b   restaurant
c   bank

Worth knowing

Tokyo, the capital of Japan, is also the cultural,
political and commercial centre of the country.
Administratively, Tokyo comprises 23
metropolitan wards, satellite cities and a number
of islands in the nearby Pacific Ocean. It is an
enormous city and close on 30 million people live
within a 30-mile radius of the centrally-sited
Imperial Palace.

Despite its size, Tokyo is relatively easy to get around and Japan's low crime rate makes it a remarkably safe city to explore. A network of subways and surface trains crisscrosses the central areas and all stations are marked well with their names in English and Japanese.

Subways Tokyo's subway network is extensive and connects most inner districts and centres. It is fast, clean and safe and is probably the most convenient way of getting around the city, but it should be avoided during the busy rush hours. Tickets are obtained from vending machines but, except at certain central stations, the destination fares are shown only in Japanese. If you can't find a fare table in English, simply buy the cheapest ticket indicated on the ticket machine and pay the difference at your destination.

The Yamanote Loop Line This line encircles the whole of central Tokyo, connecting with many railway and subway stations. Running much of the time on elevated tracks it is an extremely useful line and affords a good way of viewing the city.

Buses The bus network in Tokyo is extensive and efficient too but information on destinations is shown only in Japanese and the complicated routes defy even residents of the city.

By now, you should know enough Japanese to be able to find your way around; to enquire whether it is the right train or right platform. But if you are in any doubt, ask any Japanese, in a friendly tone of voice, simply saying only the name of your destination station, or the line you are seeking.

6 Business and pleasure

Key expressions

How do you do?	*Hajimemashite. Dōzo yoroshiku (onegaishimasu)* (When meeting for the first time and as in English, both partners can use the same expression)
This is my business card	*meishi des* *Meishi o dōzo*
Thank you for your help	*Osewa ni narimashita*
By the way (changing the topic)	*Tokoro de*
Are you free?	*Ohima desu ka?*
How are you?	*Ogenki desu ka?*
I'm fine	*Genki desu*
With pleasure	*Yorokonde*
My regards to ...	*... ni yoroshiku*
How old is he/she?	*Nan-sai desu ka?*
Do you understand English?	*Eigo ga wakarimasu ka?*
I'm/we're having trouble	*Komatte imasu*
That's/it's a pity	*Zannen desu*

Conversations

Introductions

KAZUYA ARAKI	Hajimemashite. Watakushi, Araki Kazuya to mōshimasu.
JUNKO HONDO	Hajimemashite. Watakushi, Hondō Junko to mōshimasu.
KAZUYA ARAKI	Dōzo yoroshiku onegaishimasu.

Being introduced and exchanging business cards

MR TANAKA	Sumisu-san, uchi no shachō o goshōkai shimasu.
MR SMITH	Zehi onegaishimasu.
MR TANAKA	Shachō, kochira wa Igirisu no Sumisu-san desu.
MR SMITH	Hajimemashite. Sumisu desu. Meishi o dōzo.
MR TANAKA	Dōmo, a, bii-bii-shii no kata desu ne. Hajimemashite. Tōkyō Shinbun no Yamada desu. Meishi o dōzo.
MR SMITH	Arigatō gozaimasu.

Mr Smith thanks Mr Yamada, the company president, for his help and invites him to dinner at his hotel

MR SMITH	Kyō wa taihen osewa ni narimashita.
MR YAMADA	Dō itashimashite.
MR SMITH	Tokoro de, ashita ohima desu ka?
MR YAMADA	Ē, yotei wa arimasen ga.
MR SMITH	Okusama to goyūshoku ni irasshaimasen ka?
MR YAMADA	Arigatō gozaimasu. Yorokonde mairimasu. Nan-ji goro ga yoroshii desu ka?
MR SMITH	Shichi-ji wa ikaga desu ka?
MR YAMADA	Kekkō desu.
MR SMITH	Jā, robii de matte imasu.

An invitation by telephone to go to Kamakura

JUNKO HONDO	Moshi, moshi
KAZUYA ARAKI	Moshi, moshi. Hondō-san desu ka?
JUNKO HONDO	Hai, sō desu.
KAZUYA ARAKI	Araki desu ga.
JUNKO HONDO	A, Araki san. Konnichi wa.
KAZUYA ARAKI	Konnichi wa. Ogenki desu ka?
JUNKO HONDO	Genki desu yo.
KAZUYA ARAKI	Tokoro de, kore kara, Kamakura e ikimasen ka?

| JUNKO HONDO | Sore wa suteki ne. |
| KAZUYA ARAKI | Jā, sugu omukae ni ikimasu. |

You are invited into someone's home

GUEST	Konban wa.
HOST	Yoku irasshaimashita. Dōzo oagari kudasai.
GUEST	Shitsurei itashimasu. Koko de kutsu o nugimasu ka?
HOST	Ē sumimasen ga ... Surippa o dōzo.
GUEST	Arigatō gozaimasu.

Do you have children?

HOST	Okosan wa irasshaimasu ka?
GUEST	Ē, otoko no ko to onna no ko to futari imasu.
HOST	Nan-sai desu ka?
GUEST	Jū-go-sai to jissai desu.

And how's business?

| GUEST | Saikin keiki wa dō desu ka? |
| HOST | Ma mā desu. En-daka de sukoshi komatte imasu. |

Your Japanese is good!

HOST	Nihongo ga jōzu desu ne.
GUEST	Iie, amari jōzu ja arimasen. Heta desu.
HOST	Iie, jōzu desu yo.

Farewell

GUEST	Mō kaerimasu.
HOST	Mā, mō sukoshi.
GUEST	Ashita hayai desu kara.
HOST	Sō desu ka? Zannen desu ne. Okusama ni yoroshiku otsutae kudasai.
GUEST	Hai, dōmo arigatō. Shitsurei shimasu.
HOST	Mata dōzo.

Vocabulary

kodomo *child, my/our child*

okosan *your child* (also *his child* etc., but not *my child*)

otoko no ko *boy*

onna no ko *girl*

goshujin *your husband*

shujin *my husband*

okusan, okusama *your wife*

shachō *president* (of a company)

keiki *business* (as in 'business is good' etc), *business conditions*

hima, ohima *free time*

shōkai, goshōkai (polite) *introduction*

yotei *plans, arrangements, commitments*

shitsurei *breach of courtesy, rudeness*

kutsu *shoes*

surippa *slippers*

endaka *the high yen, high exchange rate of the yen*

meishi *name card, business card*

pātii *party*

sewa, osewa *care*

robii *lobby*

yūshoku, goyūshoku *evening meal*

... goro *about ...* (referring to time)

dō? *how?*

... ga *... but*

mō *now, one more, already*

kyō *today*

ashita *tomorrow*

taihen *very*

amari *not very*

-sai *... years old*

mata *again*

jōzu *good at*

heta *poor at, bad at*

ii, yoroshii (formal) *good*

suteki *wonderful*

watakushi, watashi *I*

uchi no *my, our*

imasu, irasshaimasu (polite) *be, exist* (referring to people/animals)

arimasu, gozaimasu (polite) *be, exist* (referring to things)

narimasu *become*

ikimasu *go*

irasshaimasu (polite) *go, come*

mairimasu (humble) *go, come*

kimasu *come*

mairimasu (humble) *come*

hajimemasu *begin*

tsutaemasu *convey, give* (a message)

agarimasu *go up*

nugimasu *take off* (shoes etc.)

wakarimasu *understand*

machimasu *wait*

shimasu, itashimasu (humble) *do*

iimasu, mōshimasu (humble) *say, name* (verb)

kaerimasu *return, go home*

mukaemasu *meet*

moshi moshi *hello*

Explanations

Araki Kazuya to mōshimasu

In Japanese it is usual practice to say the family name first and then (if you wish) the given name.

It's also normal practice for people to call each other by the family name, not the given name, however close the friendship may be. Remember that you cannot use -*san* when referring to yourself.

(name) to mōshimasu I am called (name)

to mōshimasu is used in very polite speech, but *only* when the speaker is talking about himself. The *to* signals reporting or quoting, in this case, the speaker's name.

Watakushi, Araki Kazuya to mōshimasu =
Watakushi wa Araki Kazuya to mōshimasu

Note wa (to mark the topic) is very often omitted in conversation.

Dōzo yoroshiku – means, literally, 'Please treat me well', but can also mean 'Please favour me'.

Irasshaimasu means the same as either *ikimasu*, or *kimasu*, or *imasu* (i.e. either *go*, or *come*, or *be*). The difference is that by using *irasshaimasu* the speaker indicates that he respects the person he is talking about. You cannot use *irasshaimasu* of yourself, your own family, etc.

Mairimasu also means either *go* or *come*, and is used in very polite speech, but *only* when the speaker is talking about himself, his family, etc. Just as *irasshaimasu* implies an attitude of respect or honour for the subject of the verb, so *mairimasu* implies disparagement of self.

Ohima desu ka?

'Are you free' literally means 'Is it free time?' The prefix *o-* in *ohima* indicates that the question is about *your* free time. A straightforward answer to this question would be *Hai, hima desu*, or *Iie, hima ja arimasen*.

desu, which is explained in Chapter 1, becomes *ja arimasen,* in negative senses.

Nan-ji goro ga yoroshii desu ka?
'What time should we come?'

Literally it means 'what time is/will be good?' Frequently *ii* is used instead of *yoroshii,* e.g. *Nan-ji goro ga ii desu ka?*

Genki desu yo **'I'm fine'**
Jōzu desu yo **'You are good at it'**

The *yo* at the end indicates that the speaker is positive, confident, about his/her statement. In English this would be indicated by the tone of voice, but the Japanese have a word for it – *yo.*

Sore wa suteki ne
'That would be very nice, wouldn't it?'

This is the shortened form of *Sore wa suteki desu ne.*

Women often drop *desu* and place more emphasis on *ne.*

Omukae ni ikimasu
'I'll go to meet/pick up someone'

The form *omukae* is derived from the core of *mukaemasu* (to meet, will meet) with the prefix *o.* This core of a verb can indicate the purpose of 'going' when it is followed by *ni ikimasu,* e.g.

mukae ni ikimasu	*to go to meet*
tabe ni ikimasu	*to go (out) to eat*
mi ni ikimasu	*to go to see*

Yoku irasshaimashita **'welcome'**

This is said to an expected guest on his/her arrival. It cannot be used as an invitation like *irasshaimase.*

Oagari kudasai 'do come in' or 'do come up'

There is always a step up (in a modern apartment it may be a very small step) from the floor of the porch/entrance area to the living area. When entering the living area, shoes should be removed and left at the lower level.

More about polite requests

machimasu	to wait
matte kudasai	*'please wait'*
omachi kudasai	*'could you wait, please'*

In the same way, with *agarimasu* – 'to come up/go up', you can say *agatte kudasai,* or politely and, to a guest, correctly, *oagari kudasai.*

otsutae kudasai	*'give (my regards ...)'*
tsutaemasu	*to give/convey* (a message, etc.)
tsutaete kudasai	*give/please give*

But this is rather abrupt. It might be appropriate if, for example, the speaker was obviously senior in rank to the other. The more formal and polite phrase is
Okusama ni yoroshiku otsutae kudasai.

Final *ga*

The *ga* at the end of a sentence means 'but', and is very often used to add a touch of uncertainty or hesitation, making the sentence less emphatic, more polite.

Koko de kutsu o nugimasu ka?
('Do I take my shoes off here?')

Ē, sumimasen ga ...
('Yes, if you wouldn't mind ...')

Ashita ohima desu ka?
('Are you free tomorrow?')

Ē, yotei wa arimasen ga ...
('Yes, I have no commitments, but ...')

Nihongo ga jōzu desu

'My/your/his/her Japanese is good'
'I am/you are/he is/she is good at Japanese'

In a negative sentence you say:

Nihongo ga jōzu ja arimasen
'I am/you are/he is/she is not good at
Japanese'
or
Nihongo ga amari jōzu ja arimasen
'I am/you are/he is/she is/not so good at Japanese'
Note Amari with negative verb (*arimasen*) means
'not very'.

Mō kaerimasu

In this context, *mō* means 'now'.

Exercises 6

1 **Make appropriate responses to the following:**

a *Hajimemashite. Hondō desu. Dōzo yoroshikū:*

b When someone thanks you for your help, *Kyō wa taihen osewa ni narimashita:*

c When someone asks how you are,
  Ogenki desu ka?

i I'm fine

ii I'm so-so

iii No, I'm not well

d When someone says your Japanese is good,
  Nihongo ga jōzu desu ne:

i No, it's not so good

ii No, I'm poor at it

e When someone asks if you understand Japanese, *Nihongo ga wakarimasu ka?*

i A little

ii No, I don't

f When someone asks how business is, *Keiki wa dō desu ka?*

i It's so-so

ii It's good

iii It's bad

g When someone says they have to go, *Mō kaerimasu:*

Stay a little longer

h When someone invites you to go to Kamakura, *Kamakura e ikimasen ka?*

i That would be a good idea

ii That would be very nice

iii With pleasure

i When someone asks if you are available to do something, *Ohima desu ka?*

i Yes, I am

ii Yes, I've no commitments

iii Sorry, but (I'm not)

2 Replace one word from the sentence *Nihongo ga jōzu desu* with each of the following words and so create four different sentences.

a Eigo   c deshita

b heta   d wa

3 Replace one word from the sentence *Okusama to goyūshoku ni irasshaimasen ka?* with:

a goshujin   c pātii

b okosan   d Kamakura

4 What do you say?

a   When you leave a room

b   When you give your regards to your friend's father

c   When you answer the telephone

d   When you present your business card

e   When you ask what time would be convenient

f   When you welcome your guest

g   When you express your disappointment

h   When you ask how old a child is

Worth knowing

Business and social meetings in Japan provide an occasion for the exchange of many polite greetings and courtesies, most of which are covered in this book.

In most business meetings, an important pre-requisite is the exchanging of name cards as part of the formal introduction. Most Japanese, especially those in business, carry name cards and they are readily offered at every suitable opportunity, and whilst it is not essential that you have a similar card to offer in return, it is certainly a useful and highly regarded method of introducing yourself. A name card is all the more welcomed if it is printed in Japanese as well as English (Japan Air Lines offer a name card printing service and will arrange delivery to a selection of hotels in Tokyo) and offered in typical Japanese fashion, that is presented in both hands in such a way that the recipient can read your name as they accept it.

If you are fortunate enough to be invited into a Japanese home remember to remove your shoes upon entering and to take your lead, in terms of conversation and hospitality, from your hosts. The Japanese are generous hosts and guests frequently give presents (a bunch of flowers or something similar) on arrival as a mark of their respect and gratitude.

The observation of such customs and practices, together with an appreciation of the Japanese language and the part that polite consideration plays within it, can add greatly to a stay in Japan.

Can you 'GET BY'?

Answers to exercises

Chapter 1

1 a Pasupōto desu
  b Kippu desu
  c Kore wa nan desu ka?
  d Are wa nan desu ka?

2 a Soko desu
  b Koko desu
  c Rimujin noriba wa doko desu ka?
  d Hoteru wa doko desu ka?
  e Dai-ichi Hoteru wa doko desu ka?
  f Tōkyō Tawā wa doko desu ka?
  g Koko desu
  h Soko desu

3 a Dai-ichi Hoteru made onegaishimasu
  b Tōkyō Tawā made onegaishimasu
  c Narita Kūkō made onegaishimasu

4 a Chekkuauto wa nan-ji desu ka?
  b Yūshoku wa nan-ji desu ka?
  c nan-ji
  d wa
  e desu
  f choshoku

Chapter 2

1 a Kōcha ni shimasu
  b Orenji-jūsu ni shimasu
  c Tōsuto ni shimasu
  d Biiru ni shimasu

2 a Kōcha (o) kudasai
  b Orenji-jūsu (o) kudasai
  c Tōsuto (o) kudasai
  d Osake (o) kudasai
  e Biiru (o) kudasai

NB *'o' is frequently omitted in conversation. See explanations Chapter 2.*

3 a Kōcha onegaishimasu
  b Orenji-jūsu onegaishimasu
  c Tōsuto onegaishimasu
  d Osake onegaishimasu
  e Biiru onegaishimasu

Chapter 2 continued

4   a   Sumimasen. Kōcha o mō ippai onegaishimasu
    b   Sumimasen. Orenji-jūsu o mō ippai onegaishimasu
    c   Sumimasen. Biiru o mō ippai onegaishimasu

5   a   Osake ga ii desu
    b   Kōhii ga ii desu
    c   Kōcha ga ii desu
    d   Rimujin ga ii desu

6   a   Ē, daisuki desu
    b   Iie, kirai desu
    c   Ē, daisuki desu
    d   Iie, kirai desu

7   a   Sumimasen ga, nomimasen
    b   Sumimasen ga, nomimasen
    c   Sumimasen ga, tabemasen
    d   Sumimasen ga, tabemasen

8   a   Ē, nomimashō
    b   Ē, nomimashō
    c   Ē, tabemashō
    d   Ē, tabemashō

Chapter 3

1   a   Pondo o en ni kaete kudasai
    b   Doru o en ni kaete kudasai
    c   Hyaku-pondo o en ni kaete kudasai
    d   Go-hyaku doru o en ni kaete kudasai
    e   Toraberāzu-chekku o en ni kaete kudasai

2   a   Kimono wa doko de utte imasu ka?
    b   Kamera wa doko de utte imasu ka?

    c   Kippu wa doko de utte imasu ka?
    d   Fuirumu wa doko de utte imasu ka?
    e   Nekkuresu wa doko de utte imasu ka?

3   a   Tokei o misete kudasai
    b   Kore o misete kudasai

    c   Ano kamera o misete kudasai
    d   Sono nekkuresu o misete kudasai
    e   Ano kimono o misete kudasai
    f   Kono yubiwa o misete kudasai

4   a   Motto chiisai no wa arimasen ka?
    b   Motto ōkii no wa arimasen ka?
    c   Motto yasui no wa arimasen ka?
    d   Motto takai no wa arimasen ka?

5   a   Kimono wa doko de utte imasu ka?
    b   Ano kimono o misete kudasai
    c   Motto yasui no wa arimasen ka?

Chapter 4

1 a Kyōto e ikitai no desu
   b Ginza e ikitai no desu
   c Hiroshima e ikitai no desu

2 a Tsugi no kado o hidari ni magatte kudasai
   b Tsugi no kado o migi ni magatte kudasai
   c Soko o hidari ni magatte kudasai
   d Soko o migi ni magatte kudasai
   e Ano kado o hidari ni magatte kudasai
   f Ano kado o migi ni magatte kudasai

3 a Ōsaka-yuki no kippu o ichi-mai onegaishimasu
   b Kōbe-yuki no kippu o ichi-mai onegaishimasu
   c Hiroshima-yuki no kippu o ichi-mai onegaishimasu
   d Fukuoka-yuki no kippu o ichi-mai onegaishimasu

4 a Denwa ga arimasu ka?
   b Terebi ga arimasu ka?
   c Shinbun ga arimasu ka?
   d Rajio ga arimasu ka?
   e Shawā ga arimasu ka?

5 a Kōhii wa ippai ikura desu ka?
   b Kippu wa ichi-mai ikura desu ka?
   c Kimono wa ichi-mai ikura desu ka?
   d Rimujin no kippu wa ichi-mai ikura desu ka?

6 a Itte kimasu
   b Tadaima

Chapter 5

1 a Kamakura e ikimasen ka?
   b Eiga e ikimasen ka?
   c Sukii e ikimasen ka?

2 a Tabemasen ka?
   b Nomimasen ka?
   c Mimasen ka?

3 a Chikatetsu ga ichiban hayai desu
   b Chikatetsu ga ichiban chikai desu
   c Chikatetsu ga ichiban yasui desu

4 a Aruite juppun desu
   b Aruite yon-pun desu
   c Aruite ni-fun desu

5 a Eki kara hoteru made dono gurai kakarimasu ka?
   b Koko kara soko made dono gurai kakarimasu ka?
   c Otera kara eki made dono gurai kakarimasu ka?

Chapter 5 continued

6   a   Osake o nomanai de kudasai
    b   Eiga o minai de kudasai
    c   Sashimi o tabenai de kudasai

7   a   Depāto wa aite imasu ka?
    b   Resutoran wa aite imasu ka?
    c   Ginkō wa aite imasu ka?

Chapter 6

1   a   Hajimemashite. *(Your surname)* desu. Dōzo yoroshiku
    b   Dō itashimashite
    c   *i* Hai, genki desu *ii* Hai, mā mā desu *iii* Iie genki ja arimasen
    d   *i* Iie, amari jōzu ja arimasen *ii* Iie, heta desu
    e   *i* Sukoshi *ii* Iie, wakarimasen
    f   *i* Mā mā desu *ii* Ii desu *iii* Dame desu
    g   Mā, mō sukoshi
    h   *i* Sore wa ii kangae desu *ii* Sore wa suteki desu *iii* Yorokonde
    i   *i* Ē, hima desu *ii* Ē, yotei wa arimasen *iii* Iie, zannen desu ga
          … hima ja arimasen

2   a   Eigo ga jōzu desu
    b   Nihongo ga heta desu
    c   Nihongo ga jōzu deshita
    d   Nihongo wa jōzu desu

3   a   Goshujin to goyūshoku ni irasshaimasen ka?
    b   Okosan to goyūshoku ni irasshaimasen ka?
    c   Okusama to pātii ni irasshaimasen ka?
    d   Okusama to Kamakura ni irasshaimasen ka?

4   a   Shitsurei shimasu
    b   Otōsama ni yoroshiku
    c   Moshi, moshi
    d   Meishi o dōzo
    e   Nan-ji ga yoroshii desu ka?
    f   Yoku irasshaimashita
    g   Zannen desu
    h   Nan-sai desu ka?

Reference section

Numbers and Counting

As explained on pages 32 and 33, there are two main systems for counting:

The *hitotsu, futatsu, mittsu* system, which is a simple method of counting things but only goes up to ten, and

the abstract number system, *ichi* (1), *ni* (2), *san* (3) (used to number the pages of this book), which, in modified form, is used in conjunction with a range of 'counters' There are many 'counters' in this system; here are some in everyday use.

People -*nin*

How many people? *Nan-nin?*

1 person	*hitori*	8 people	*hachi-nin*
2 people	*futari*	9 people	*kyū-nin*
3 people	*san-nin*	10 people	*jū-nin*
4 people	*yo-nin*	11 people	*jū-ichi-nin*
5 people	*go-nin*	12 people	*jū-ni-nin*
6 people	*roku-nin*		
7 people	*shichi-nin/nana-nin*		

Liquid measures (glassful, cupful) -*hai*/-*bai*/-*pai*

How many glasses/cups? *Nan-bai?*

1 glassful	*ippai*	8 glassfuls	*hachi-hai*
2 glassfuls	*ni-hai*	9 glassfuls	*kyū-hai*
3 glassfuls	*san-bai*	10 glassfuls	*juppai*
4 glassfuls	*yon-hai*	11 glassfuls	*jū-ippai*
5 glassfuls	*go-hai*	12 glassfuls	*jū-ni-hai*
6 glassfuls	*roppai*		
7 glassfuls	*shichi-hai/nana-hai*		

Paper, plates
(flat objects) *mai*

How many? *Nan-mai?*

1 paper	*ichi-mai*
2 papers	*ni-mai*
3 papers	*san-mai*
4 papers	*yon-mai*
5 papers	*go-mai*
6 papers	*roku-mai*
7 papers	*shichi-mai/* *nana-mai*
8 papers	*hachi-mai*
9 papers	*kyū-mai*
10 papers	*jū-mai*
11 papers	*jū-ichi-mai*
12 papers	*jū-ni-mai*

Pencils, trees, bottles
(slender objects) *-hon*

How many? *Nan-bon?*

1 pencil	*ippon*
2 pencils	*ni-hon*
3 pencils	*san-bon*
4 pencils	*yon-hon*
5 pencils	*go-hon*
6 pencils	*roppon*
7 pencils	*shichi-hon/* *nana-hon*
8 pencils	*hachi-hon/* *happon*
9 pencils	*kyū-hon*
10 pencils	*juppon/jippon*
11 pencils	*jū-ippon*
12 pencils	*jū-ni-hon*

Floors of a building -kai/-gai

Which/How many floors? *Nan-gai?*

1st floor	*ikkai*	8th floor	*hachi-kai*
2nd floor	*ni-kai*	9th floor	*kyū-kai*
3rd floor	*san-gai*	10th floor	*jukkai/jikkai*
4th floor	*yon-kai*	11th floor	*jū-ikkai*
5th floor	*go-kai*	12th floor	*jū-ni-kai*
6th floor	*rokkai*		
7th floor	*shichi-kai/nana-kai*		

Time

-pun, -fun minutes

1 ippun	15 jū-go-fun
2 ni-fun	16 jū-roppun
3 san-pun	17 jū-nana-fun/shichi-fun
4 yon-pun	18 jū-hachi-fun
5 go-fun	19 jū-kyū-fun
6 roppun	20 ni-jippun/juppun
7 nana-fun/shichi-fun	25 ni-jū-go-fun
8 hachi-fun	30 san-juppun
9 kyū-fun	35 san-jū-go-fun
10 jippun/juppun	40 yon-juppun
11 jū-ippun	45 yon-jū-go-fun
12 jū-ni-fun	50 go-juppun
13 jū-san-pun	55 go-jū-go-fun
14 jū-yon-fun	60 roku-juppun

ji hours

1.00 a.m.	ichi-ji	7.00	shichi-ji/nana-ji
2.00 a.m.	ni-ji	8.00	hachi-ji
3.00 a.m.	san-ji	9.00	ku-ji
4.00 a.m.	yo-ji	10.00	jū-ji
5.00 a.m.	go-ji	11.00	jū-ichi-ji
6.00 a.m.	roku-ji	12.00	jū-ni-ji

Days

Sunday	*nichi-yōbi*
Monday	*getsu-yōbi*
Tuesday	*ka-yōbi*
Wednesday	*sui-yōbi*
Thursday	*moku-yōbi*
Friday	*kin-yōbi*
Saturday	*do-yōbi*

Months

In Japanese, months are literally called first month, second month, third month and so on, and they correspond to the Gregorian calendar months January, February, March etc.

January	*Ichigatsu*
February	*Nigatsu*
March	*Sangatsu*
April	*Shigatsu*
May	*Gogatsu*
June	*Rokugatsu*
July	*Shichigatsu*
August	*Hachigatsu*
September	*Kugatsu*
October	*Jūgatsu*
November	*Jūichigatsu*
December	*Jūnigatsu*

Seasons

Spring	*Haru*
Summer	*Natsu*
Autumn	*Aki*
Winter	*Fuyu*

Directions

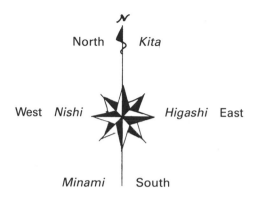

North **Kita**

West **Nishi** — **Higashi** East

Minami South

Useful addresses and telephone numbers

JAPAN NATIONAL TOURIST OFFICE
167 Regent Street, London W1R 7FD
Tel. (01) 734 9638

Offers an information service, pamphlets and maps for prospective visitors to Japan. They also sell the Japan Rail Pass which enables unlimited travel on the Japan National Railways for periods of 7, 14 or 21 days and must be bought outside Japan.

JAPAN NATIONAL TOURIST ORGANISATION
6-6 Yuraku-cho 1-chome, Chiyoda-ku, Tokyo
Tel. (03) 502 1461

NEW TOKYO INTERNATIONAL AIRPORT (NARITA)
Airport Terminal Building, Narita
Chiba prefecture, 286-11
Tel. (0476) 32 8711

KYOTO TOURIST INFORMATION
Kyoto Tower Building, Higashi-shiokojicho
Shimogyo-ku, Kyoto, 600
Tel. (075) 371 5649

The above three tourist information centres cater specifically for overseas visitors, although most towns and cities have information centres supplying some information in English.

JAPAN TRAVEL PHONE

This service provides English language assistance and travel information, toll-free, for those who've ventured outside the main centres of Tokyo or Kyoto. Simply dial 106 and say 'Collect call T.I.C. please'. Within the city limits of Tokyo or Kyoto, contact the appropriate tourist office.

TELETOURIST SERVICE

This gives taped information on current events in Tokyo.
Tel. (03) 265 5511

PLAY GUIDE HONTEN

2-6-4 Ginza, Chuo-ku, Tokyo
Tel. (03) 561 8821

Contact the Play Guide head office in Ginza or one of its many branches for tickets for traditional Japanese theatre, cinema and sporting events.

TOKYO TELEGRAPH OFFICE

8-1 Otemachi 1-chome, Tokyo
Tel. (03) 211 5588

Open 24 hours a day for telegrams, facsimiles, phototelegrams, international phone calls and telexes.

There are also many special green pay phones displaying an 'INTERNATIONAL TELEPHONE' sign. To make an overseas call, either insert 100 yen coins or use a telephone card (available from kiosks) and dial 001 + country code + area code + number.

For information on international phone calls, contact the *KDD Information Centre (03) 270 5111.*

BRITISH EMBASSY

No. 1, 1-1 Ban cho, Chiyoda-ku, Tokyo
Tel. (03) 265 5511

BRITISH COUNCIL

2 Kagurasaka 1-chome, Shinjuku-ku, Tokyo 162
Tel. (03) 235 8031

Word list

The following is an alphabetical list of all the words appearing in the six chapters.

A

a *oh!*
ā *oh! ah! well*
achira *over there*
agarimasu *go up*
aite (imasu) (verb *aku*) *(is) open*
aki *autumn*
amai *sweet*
amari (plus negative) *not so, not very*
annaisho *guide book*
ano *that over there*
are *that over there*
arigatō *thank you*
arimasen *have not*
arimasu *have (referring to things)*
aruite (verb *aruku*) *walk*
asa *morning*
Asakusa *place name in Tokyo*
ashita *tomorrow*
asoko *over there, that place over there*
atarashii *new*

B

basu *bus*
benri *convenient*
biiru *beer*

C

chekku *cheque* (toraberāzu-chekku) *(traveller's cheque)*
chekkuauto *check-out*
chiisai *small*
chikai *near*
chikatetsu *underground*

chōdo *just, exactly*
chōshoku *breakfast* (chōshoku-tsuki) *breakfast included*
chotto *a little*
Chūka ryōri *Chinese food*

D

daisuki *like a lot*
dame *no good*
de *by, with, at*
deguchi *exit*
demashita (verb *deru*) *left*
densha *train*
denwa *telephone*
desu *is, are etc.*
desu kara *therefore*
dewa *then*
dō *how*
dō itashimashite *you're welcome, don't mention it*
dō nasaimasu ka? *what will you do?* (very polite)
do shimasu ka *what will you do?*
dobutsu-en *zoo*
dochira *which*
doko *where*
dōmo *thanks*
(dōmo arigatō) *thank you very much*
donata *who*
dono *how*
(dono gurai) *how much (time or distance)*
doru *dollar*
dōshite *why*
dōzo *please (go ahead)*

E

e *to, toward*

ē   *yes*
(ē so desu)   *yes, that's right*
eiga   *film, movie*
eigakan   *cinema*
eigo   *English*
eki   *station*
en   *yen*
endaka   *high exchange rate of yen*
erebētā   *lift, elevator*
esukarētā   *escalator*

F

ferii   *ferryboat*
fōku   *fork*
fuirumu   *film*
fune   *ship*
Furansu ryōri   *French food*
(o)furo   *bath*
furui   *old*
futari   *two people*
fuyu   *winter*

G

ga   *but*
ga   *indicates subject*
-gai   *floor*
(san-gai)   *third floor*
gaika   *foreign currency*
garō   *art gallery*
gekijō   *theatre*
(o)genki (desu ka?)   *how are you?*
genkin   *cash*
ginkō   *bank*
Ginza   *place name in Tokyo*
Ginza-sen   *Ginza line*
gochisō   *feast*
gochisōsama   *a good meal*
(gochisōsama deshita)   *thank you for the meal*
go   *five*
(go-fun)   *five minutes*
(go-jū-en)   *fifty yen*
(go-sen-en)   *five thousand yen*

goro   *about* (referring to time)
goshujin   *your husband*
gozen   *morning, a.m.*
gurai   *about*

H

hade   *loud* (colour)
hagaki   *postcard*
hai   *yes*
haikanryō   *entrance fee*
hajimemashite   *how do you do?*
hajimemasu   *begin*
hajimete   *first time*
hakubutsukan   *museum*
haru   *spring*
(o)hashi   *chopsticks*
hatsu   *departure*
hayai   *fast, early*
heta   *bad, poor*
(o)heya   *room*
hidari   *left*
hikōki   *aeroplane*
(o)hima   *free time*
hiroi   *wide*
hitoban   *one night*
(o)hitori   *one person*
hitotsu   *one*
hōmu   *platform*
hoshii   *want*
hoteru   *hotel*
hyaku (pondo)   *one hundred (pounds)*

I

ichiba   *market*
ichiban   *first*
ichi-mai   *one* (flat object)
ichiman   *ten thousand*
(ichiman-go-sen)   *fifteen thousand*
(ichiman en satsu)   *ten thousand yen note*
Igirisu   *England*

ii *good*
iie *no*
iimasu *say, name*
ikaga *how is it?*
ikimashō (verb *iku*) *let's go*
ikimasu (verb *iku*) *go*
ikitai (verb *iku*) *want to go*
ikkai *first floor*
ikura *how much, many*
imasu *be, exist* (referring to people/animals)
ippai *one cup, glassful*
irasshaimase *welcome*
irimasen (verb *iru*) *do not need*
irimasu *need, want*
itadakimasu *receive, will receive* – said before eating (polite, humble)
itte (verb *iku*) *go* (imperative)
itte irasshaimase *said to person leaving a house, hotel etc.*
itte kimasu *said when leaving a house, hotel etc.*
ittō *first class*

J

jā *well then*
jā mata *see you soon*
jamu *jam*
-ji *o'clock*
(nan-ji) *what time?*
jidōsha *car*
jimi *subdued* (colour)
jinja *shrine*
jissai *ten years old*
jitensha *bicycle*
jiyū-seki *unreserved seat*
jōsha-ken *ordinary ticket*
jōzu *clever, good*
jū *ten*
jū-ichi *eleven*
jū-ji *10 o'clock*
jū-san-ji *13 hours, 1 o'clock*

jū-kyū-ban-sen *platform 19*
jū-yon-ban-sen *platform 14*
jūsu *juice*

K

ka *question form*
kaemasu (verb *kaeru*) *change*
kaerimashō (verb *kaeru*) *let's go home*
kaerimasu *return, go home*
(o)kaerinasai *welcome back* (home etc.)
kaete (verb *kaeru*) *change* (imperative)
kaidan *stairs*
kaimashō (verb *kau*) *let's buy*
kaite (verb *kaku*) *write* (imperative)
kakarimasu (verb *kakaru*) *take* (time), *cost* (money)
Kamakura *place name*
kamera *camera*
kangae *thought*
(o)kanjō *bill*
kanpai *cheers*
kantan *easy*
kara *from*
(sore kara) *then*
karui *light*
kata *person*
katamichi *one way*
katarogu *catalogue*
katte (verb *kau*) *buy* (imperative)
keiki *business*
kēki *cake*
kekkō desu *it's fine etc.*
kimasu *come*
kimono *kimono*
kin-en-sha *non-smoking car*
kippu *ticket*
kirai *don't like*
kirei *pretty*
kissaten *coffee shop*

kitanai *dirty*
kitte *stamp*
ko *child*
kōcha *black tea*
kochira (e) *this way*
kodomo *children*
kōen *park*
kōhii *coffee*
koko *here, this place*
Kōkyo *Imperial Palace*
komarimashita (verb komaru) *I was having trouble*
komatte imasu *I'm having trouble*
konban *this evening*
konban wa *good evening*
konnichi wa *good afternoon*
kono *this*
konsāto-hōru *concert hall*
kore *this*
kōsaten *crossroads, junction*
koshō *pepper*
ku *nine*
(ku-ji) *9 o'clock*
kudasai *please* (polite request)
kūkō *airport*
kuruma *car*
kutsu *shoes*
(o)kyaku-san *customer*
kyō *today*
Kudamono *fruit*

M

machi *town*
machimasu *wait*
made *until, up to*
magatte (verb magaru) *turn* (imperative)
-mai *counter* (for flat things)
mairimasu *come* (very polite)
massugu *straight ahead*
mata *again, soon*
(o)matase *wait*

matte (verb matsu) *wait* (imperative)
mayoimashita (verb mayou) *was lost*
meishi *name card*
menyū *menu*
michi *road*
migi *right*
mijikai *short*
miruku *milk*
mise *shop*
misemasu (verb miseru) *show*
misete (verb miseru) *show* (imperative)
mitai (verb miru) *want to see*
(o)miyage *souvenir*
(o)mizu *water*
mo *also, too*
mō *again, already, now*
(mō ichido) *once again*
(mō ippai) *one more cup*
mochiron *of course*
mono *thing*
mōshimasu *I'm called* (very polite)
moshi moshi *hello* (telephone)
motto *more*
mukae *meet*
(mukae ni ikimasu) *go and meet*
mukaemasu *meet*

N

nagai *long*
naifu *knife*
naito kurabu *night club*
naka *inside*
nan *what*
nan-ji *what time*
nan-sai *how old*
nana *seven*
nana-man *seventy thousand*

narimashita (verb *naru*) *became*

narimasu *become*

(osewa ni narimashita) *thank you for your help*

nasaimasu *do* (very polite)

natsu *summer*

ne sentence ending asking for agreement – *isn't it?*

nekkuresu *necklace*

ni *two*

nichiyōbi *Sunday*

ni-hai *two cups*

Nihon *Japan*

Nihon ryōri *Japanese food*

niku *meat*

ni-mai *two flat things*

ni-man *twenty thousand*

(o)nimotsu *luggage*

Nippon *Japan*

nitō *second class*

no *of*

nomimasu (verb *nomu*) *drink, will drink*

(o)nomimono *a drink*

nonde (verb *nomu*) *drink* (imperative)

noriba *stop* (e.g. bus *stop*)

norikae *change* (e.g. trains)

notte (verb *noru*) *ride* (imperative)

nugimasu *take off* (shoes etc.)

O

o *indicates direct object*

obi *sash worn with kimono*

ocha *green tea*

ōfuku *return ticket*

ohayō (gozaimasu) *good morning*

oishii *delicious*

ōkii *big*

okosan *your child* (also *his child* etc., but not *my* child)

okusan *your wife*

okyaku-san *client, customer*

omawari-san *policeman*

omoi *heavy*

onegaishimasu *please (do me a favour)*

onna no ko *girl*

orenji (-jūsu) *orange (juice)*

oshio *salt*

otoko no ko *boy*

otona *adult*

oyasumi (nasai) *goodnight*

P

pasupōto *passport*

pātii *party*

pondo *pound*

R

rajio *radio*

rāmen *noodles*

remon *lemon*

remon tii *lemon tea*

resutoran *restaurant*

rimujin *limousine*

robii *lobby*

rōka *corridor*

roku-ji *6 o'clock*

ryokan *Japanese-style hotel*

ryōri *food*

ryōshūsho *receipt*

S

sai (nan-sai) *years old (how old?)*

saikin *recently*

sakana *fish*

(o)sake *rice wine*

(o)saki ni *I'm going first*

-sama *Mr, Mrs, Miss, Ms*

(gochisōsama deshita) *thank you for the meal*

samui *cold*

san *Mr*

san *three*

san-bai *three glasses*

san-gai *third floor*
sarada *salad*
(o)sashimi *raw fish*
(o)satō *sugar*
satsu *note* (money)
sayōnara *goodbye*
semai *narrow, small*
sen *line* (train)
sen *thousand*
(o)sewa *care*
shachō *president* (of a company)
shawā *shower*
shichi *seven*
shikata *way, means*
(shikata ga arimasen) *it can't be helped*
shimarimasu (verb *shimaru*) *close*
shimasu (verb *suru*) *do, will do*
shinbun *newspaper*
shindai-sha *sleeping berth*
Shinkansen *Bullet Train*
(o)shio *salt*
shiro *castle*
shitei-seki *reserved seat*
shitsurei (shimasu) *I'm sorry, excuse me*
shōkai *introduce, introduction*
shokudō-sha *dining car*
shokuji *meal*
shōshō *a little*
shūden *last train*
shujin *my husband*
(go shujin) *someone else's husband*
soba *noodles*
sochira *that way*
sō desu *that's right*
sono *that*
soko *there, that place*
sore *that*
soretomo *or*
soto *outside*

sugu *soon*
suki *like*
sukii *ski, skiing*
sukiyaki *meat (dish)*
sukoshi *a little*
sumimasen *I'm sorry, excuse me*
Sumisu *Smith*
surippa *slippers*
sushi *vinegared rice food*
sushi-ya *sushi shop*
suteki *great, nice*
suwanai *don't smoke*

T

tabako *cigarettes*
tabako-ya *tobacconist*
tabemashō (verb *taberu*) *let's eat*
tabemasu (verb *taberu*) *eat*
tabete (verb *taberu*) *eat* (imperative)
tadaima *I'm home; immediately*
taihen *very*
takai *expensive*
takushii *taxi*
tazunemashō *let's ask*
(o)tearai *toilet*
tempura *deep fried food*
(o)tera *temple*
terebi *television*
to *and*
tōi *far*
tokei *watch*
tokkyū *super express train*
tokkyū-ken *super express ticket*
tokorode *by the way*
tōsuto *toast*
tsugi *next*
tsukiatari *end*
tsukimasu (verb *tsuku*) *arrive*
(o)tsuri *change*
tsūro *passageway*

(o)tsutae *conveying* (a
   message)
tsutaemasu *convey, give* (a
   message)

U

uchi *home*
(uchi no shachō) *our
   president*
udon *noodles*
uisukii *whisky*
uketsuke *reception*
uriba *counter*
urimasu (verb *uru*) *sell*
utte imasu *is/are sold*

W

wa *indicates topic*
wakarimasen (verb *wakaru*)
   do not understand
wakarimasu *understand*
warui *bad*
watakushi *I*
watashi *I*

Y

yakitori *barbecued chicken
   etc.*

yasai vegetable

yasui *cheap*
yo *at the end of sentence for
   emphasis*
yoku *very, often*
(yoku irasshaimashita)
   you're very welcome
... yori *(more) than* ...
yorokonde *with pleasure*
yoroshii (formal) *all right,
   good*
yoroshiku *regards*
yotei *schedule, plan,
   commitments*
yūbinkyoku *post office*
yubiwa *ring for the finger*
yukata *informal
   cotton robe*
-yuki *-bound (train etc.)*
yūshoku *evening meal*

Z

zannen *a pity*
-zen *thousand*
(san-zen-en) *three thousand
   yen*
zenbu *all*